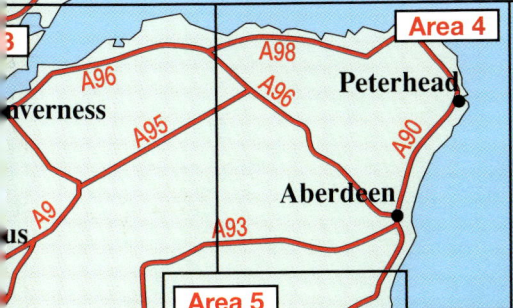

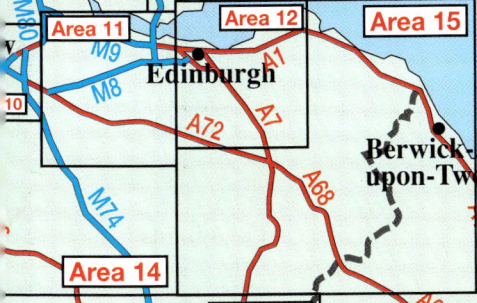

GOLF

IN

SCOTLAND

Published by Roger Kidd's Golf Guides
26 Cedar Road Sutton Surrey SM2 5DG

Practice Facilities

SECTION 3	Telephone	Bays	Floodlit
Castle Heather	01343 810061	12	✓
Lossiemouth GR	01343 820424	16	✓
Spey Bay DR	01463 713335	20	✓

SECTION 4	Telephone	Bays	Floodlit
Buchan GR	01346 561205	11	✓
East Aberdeenshire	01358 742111	16	✓
Inchmarlo GC	01330 822557	30	✓
Inverurie DR	01467 620193	15	✓
Kings Links GC	01224 641577	58	✓
Meldrum House DR	01651 873553	11	
Newmachar GC	01651 863222	24	✓

SECTION 5	Telephone	Bays	Floodlit
Ballumbie Castle DR	01382 770028	22	✓
Edzell GC	01356 647283	9	✓
Piperdam	01382 581374	14	
Middlebank GR	01821 670320	23	✓
Strathmore GC	01828 633322	10	✓

SECTION 7	Telephone	Bays	Floodlit
Crieff Hydro GC	01764 655555	8	
Forrester Park	01383 880505	20	✓
Gleneagles GC	01764 662231	24	✓
Murrayshall GR	01738 552784	19	✓
Noah's Ark	01738 440678	22	✓
Brucefields Family GC	01786 818184	26	✓

SECTION 8	Telephone	Bays	Floodlit
Scottish National GC	01382 541144	25	✓
St Andrews GPC	01334 474489	44	✓
Wellsgreen GR	01592 712435	18	✓

SECTION 9	Telephone	Bays	Floodlit
Castle Golf Range	01505 383599	20	4

SECTION 10	Telephone	Bays	Floodlit
Bearsden Golf Range	0141 942 2828	14	✓
Bishopbriggs GR	0141 762 4883	24	✓
Gary Mitchell GS	0141 641 8899	25	✓
Rouken Glen GC	0141 638 7044	15	✓
John Mulgrew EPGC	0141 886 7477	25	✓
World of Golf GR	0141 944 4141	72	✓

SECTION 11	Telephone	Bays	Floodlit
Forth View Academy	01324 831112	22	✓
Palacerigg Golf Centre	01236 737000	20	✓
Polkemmet DR	01501 743905	15	✓

SECTION 12	Telephone	Bays	Floodlit
Braid Hills GR	0131 658 1111	44	✓
Kings Acre DR	0131 663 3456	30	✓
Marriott Dalmahoy	0131 333 1845	12	✓
Melville Golf Centre	0131 663 8038	34	✓
Port Royal DR	0131 333 4377	35	✓

SECTION 13	Telephone	Bays	Floodlit
Auchenharvie GC	01294 603103	20	✓
Brunston Castle	01465 811471	10	✓
Loudon Golf Centre	01563 822061	21	✓
North Gailes GC	01294 204201	30	
Prestwick Golf Centre	01292 479849	28	✓

SECTION 14	Telephone	Bays	Floodlit
Dalziel Park Golf & GC	01698 862444	15	✓
Strathclyde GC	01698 285511	27	✓

SECTION 15	Telephone	Bays	Floodlit
Mount Hooley GR	01835 850787	16	✓
Castle Park GC	01620 810733	7	
Jane Connachan GC	01620 850475	24	✓

SECTION 16	Telephone	Bays	Floodlit
Brighouse Bay	01557 870409	6	
Park of Tongland	01556 680226	9	✓

For further information on golf visit:
www.scottishgolf.com

For tourist information visit:
www.visitscotland.com

Golf in Scotland

Golf: The flower of Scotland

Welcome to the home of golf – Scotland, where it all began over 500 years ago. Today Scotland with a population of under six million, has over 525 courses.

The period between 1890 and 1910 represented the greatest expansion in the history of Scottish golf, with over 200 courses being laid out by masters such as James Braid, Tom Morris and Willie Fernie. A latter day renaissance in the 1990s heralded the opening of many new fine courses such as The Roxburghe, Kingsbarns, St. Andrews Bay, Craigielaw and Southern Gailes.

No matter what part of the country you visit, great golf is always at hand, Macrihanish in the west, Boat of Garten nestling in the Highlands, the majesty of Royal Dornoch in the north, Cruden Bay and Crail – gems of the east, 9 hole St. Bothwells in the border counties and a personal favourite, perhaps as I caddied there as a boy, the superb Western Gailes, situated just north of the championship links of Royal Troon in Ayrshire.

Whilst some of the more famous courses can be quite expensive, Scotland in general offers great value for money, with a range of wonderful courses at very reasonable prices. From the course summaries, you will see that many are set in stunning, majestic surroundings as the scenery of Scotland is indeed truly special. So wherever you visit, be it Western Isles, Highlands, Central or Borders, you will bring back a lifetime of special memories.

Whether a fellow Scot or a welcome visitor, you will find this book an indispensable mine of essential information. So pack your clubs, wave goodbye to the family and set off on the journey of a lifetime. You will not be disappointed.

And most important of all, in the words of the great Walter Hagen, "*Take time to smell the flowers*".

Play well

Roger Kidd

CONTENTS

Course	Area No.	Course	Area No.
Esporta Douglaston	10	**H**	
Eyemouth	15	Haddington	15
		Haggs Castle	10
F		Hamilton	14
Falkirk	11	Harburn	11
Falkirk Tryst	11	Hawick	15
Falkland	8	Hayston	10
Fereneze	9	Hazelhead	4
Forfar	5	Helensburgh	9
Forres	3	Helmsdale	2
Forrester Park	7	Hilton Park	10
Fort Augustus	3	Hirsel	15
Fortrose & Rosemarkie	3	Hoddom Castle	17
Fort William	1	Hollandbush	14
Fraserburgh	4	Hopeman	3
		Huntly	4
G			
Gairloch	1	**I**	
Galashields	15	Inchmarlo	4
Garmouth & Kingston	3	Innellan	9
Gatehouse of Fleet	16	Innerleithen	15
Gifford	15	Insch	4
Gigha	6	Inverallochy	4
Girvan	13	Inveraray	6
Glasgow	10	Invergordon	2
Glasgow Gailes	13	Inverness	3
Gleddoch	9	Inverurie	4
Glen	15	Irvine	13
Glenbervie	11	Irvine Ravenspark	13
Glencorse	12	Isle of Eriska	6
Glencruiton	6	Isle of Harris	1
Gleneagles Hotel	7	Isle of Seil	6
Glenisla	5	Isle of Skye	1
Glenrothes	8		
Gogarburn	12	**J**	
Golspie	2	Jedburgh	15
Gourock	9		
Grangemouth	11	**K**	
Grantown-on-Spey	3	Keith	3
Greenburn	11	Kelso	15
Green Hotel	7	Kemnay	4
Greenock	9	Kenmore	7
Greenock Whinhill	9	Kilbirnie Place	9
Gretna	17	Killin	7
Gullane	15	Kilmacolm	9

Course	Area No.	Course	Area No.
Kilmarnock Barassie	13	Lochgoilhead	6
Kilspindie	12	Loch Lomond	9
Kilsyth Lennox	10	Lochmaben	17
Kinghorn	8	Loch Ness	3
King James VI	7	Lochore Meadows	8
Kings Acre	12	Lochranza	13
Kingsbarns	8	Lochwinnoch	9
Kingsknowe	12	Lockerbie	17
Kings Links	4	Longniddry	12
Kings Park	10	Longside	4
Kingussie	3	Lothianburn	12
Kinloss	3	Loudoun Gowf	13
Kintore	4	Luffness New	12
Kirkcaldy	8	Lumphanan	4
Kirkcudbright	16	Lundin Ladies	8
Kirkhill	10	Lundin Links	8
Kirkintilloch	10	Lybster	2
Kirriemuir	5		
Knightswood	10	**M**	
Kyles of Bute	6	Machrie	6
		Machrie Bay	13
		Machrihanish	6
L		Marriott Dalmahoy	12
Ladybank	8	Maybole	13
Lagganmore	16	McDonald	4
Lamlash	13	Meldrum House	4
Lanark	14	Melrose	15
Langholm	17	Melville	12
Langlands	14	Merchants of Edinburgh	12
Largs	9	Millport	9
Larkhall	14	Milnathort	8
Lauder	15	Milngavie	10
Leadhills	14	Minto	15
Lenzie	10	Moffat	14
Leslie	8	Monifieth	5
Letham Grange	5	Montrose	5
Lethamhill	10	Moray	3
Leven Links	8	Mortonhall	12
Liberton	12	Mount Ellen	10
Lilliardsedge	15	Mouse Valley	14
Linlithgow	11	Muckhart	7
Linn Park	10	Muirfield	15
Littlehill	10	Muirkirk	14
Lochcarron	1	Muir of Ord	3
Lochgelly	8	Murcar	4
Lochgilphead	6		

Course	Area No.	Course	Area No.
Murrayshall Hotel	7	Portpatrick	16
Murrayfield	12	Powfoot	17
Musselburgh	12	Prestonfield	12
Musselburgh Old	12	Prestwick	13
Muthill	7	Prestwick St Cuthbert	13
		Prestwick St Nicholas	13
		Pumpherston	11

N

Course	Area No.
Nairn	3
Nairn Dunbar	3
Newbattle	12
Newburgh-on-Ythan	4
Newcastleton	17
New Cumnock	14
New Galloway	16
Newmachar	4
Newtonmore	3
Newton Stewart	16
Niddry Castle	11
North Berwick	15
North Inch	7

R

Course	Area No.
Ralston	10
Ranfurly Castle	9
Ratho Park	12
Ravelston	12
Reay	2
Renfrew	10
Resipole	1
Rosehearty	4
Rothes	3
Rothesay	9
Rouken Glen	10
Routenburn	9
Roxburghe, The	15
Royal Aberdeen	4
Royal Burgess	12
Royal Dornoch	2
Royal Musselburgh	12
Royal Tarlair	4
Royal Troon	13
Rutherford Castle	15

O

Course	Area No.
Oatridge	11
Old Course Ranfurly	9
Oldmeldrum	4
Orkney	2

P

Course	Area No.
Paisley	9
Palacerigg	11
Panmure	5
Peebles	15
Peterculter	4
Peterhead	4
Pines	17
Piperdam	5
Pitlochry	3
Pitreavie	7
Polkemmet	11
Pollock	10
Polmont	11
Port Bannatyne	9
Port Glasgow	9
Portlethen	4
Portobello	12

S

Course	Area No.
St. Andrews	8
St. Andrews Bay	8
St. Boswells	15
St. Fillans	7
St. Meaden	16
St. Michaels	8
Saline	7
Sanday	2
Sandyhills	10
Sanquhar	14
Sconnie	8
Scotscraig	8
Seafield	13
Selkirk	15

Golf in Scotland

Course	Area No.	Course	Area No.
Shetland	2	Turnberry	13
Shiskine	13	Turnhouse	12
Shotts	11	Turriff	4
Silverknowes	12		
Skeabost	1	**U**	
Skelmorlie	9	Ullapool	1
Spean Bridge	1	Uphall	11
Spey Bay	3		
Solway Links	17	**V**	
Southerness	17	Vale of Leven	9
Southern Gailes	13	Vaul	6
Stirling	7	Vogrie	12
Stonehaven	5		
Stornaway	1	**W**	
Stranraer	16	Western Gailes	13
Strathaven	14	Westerwood Hotel	11
Strathclyde Park	14	Westhill	4
Strathendrick	9	West Kilbride	13
Strathlene	3	West Linton	15
Strathmore	5	West Lothian	11
Strathpeffer Spa	3	Whalsay	2
Strathtay	7	Whitecraigs	10
Stromness	2	Whitekirk	15
Swanston	12	Whitemoss	7
		Whiting Bay	13
T		Wick	2
Tain	2	Wigtown & Bladnoch	16
Tarbat	2	Wigtownshire County	16
Tarbert	6	Williamwood	10
Tarland	4	Windyhill	10
Taymouth Castle	7	Winterfield	15
Taynuilt	6	Wishaw	14
Thornhill	14	Woll	15
Thornton	8		
Thurso	2		
Tillicoultry	7		
Tobermory	6		
Torphin Hill	12		
Torphins	4		
Torrance House	14		
Torvean	3		
Torwoodlee	15		
Traigh	1		
Troon Municipals	13		
Tulliallan	7		

Area One

Askernish (1891)

Lochboisdale, Askernish, South Uist, Western Isles HS81 5ST
Tel: 01878 700398 or 700399   Fax: 01878 700309
Green Fee: ①   9 Holes   5042 yds   SSS: 67
Visitors: Anyday   Designer: Tom Morris
A links course with excellent views and ever changing conditions

Barra (1992)

Cleat, Castlebay, Isle of Barra, Western Isles HS9 5XX
Tel: 01871 810419   Fax: 01871 810418
Green Fee: ①   9 Holes   5032 yds   SSS: 64
Visitors: Anyday   Designer: Unknown
Breathtaking views of Barra beaches. Most Westerly course in Britain

Benbecula (1992)

Balivanich, Isle of Benbecula, Western Isles HS7 5LA
Tel: 01870 602467 or 602126
Green Fee: ①   9 Holes   4311 yds   SSS: 62
Visitors: Anyday   Designer: Unknown
Difficult links type course

Durness (1988)

Durness, Sutherland IV27 4PN
Tel: 01971 511364   Fax: 01971 511321
Green Fee: ①   9 Holes   5555 yds   SSS: 67
Visitors: Anyday   Designers: Keith/Ross/Morrison
Interesting seaside course with dramatic scenery

Fort William (1975)

Torlundy, Nr. Fort William, Inverness-shire PH33 6SN
Tel: 01397 704464   Fax: 01397 705893   Sec: 01397 702404
Green Fee: ①   18 Holes   6217 yds   SSS: 71
Visitors: Anyday   Designer: Hamilton Stutt
Although next to Ben Nevis (Britain's highest mountain) this moorland course is fairly flat

Gairloch (1898)

Gairloch, Ross-shire IV21 2BE
Tel: 01445 712407   Fax: 01445 712407
Green Fee: ①   9 Holes   4734 yds   SSS: 64
Visitors: Anyday   Designer: Captain Burgess
Seaside links course with marvellous views of sandy beaches and across the sea to Skye

Isle of Harris (1984)

Scarista Mhor, Isle of Harris, Western Isles HS3 3HT
Tel: 01859 502331
Green Fee: ①   9 Holes   4864 yds   SSS: 64
Visitors: Anyday (No Sunday play)   Designer: Nature
Bordered on one side by the sound of Taransay with lovely beaches to the West

Isle of Skye (1964)

Sconser, Isle of Skye, Inverness-shire IV48 8TD
Tel: 01478 650414 (Seasonal) or 613004   Fax: 01478 650351
Green Fee: ①   9 Holes   4798 yds   SSS: 64
Visitors: Anyday   Designer: Dr. F. Deighton
Seaside course with stunning views of the Cullin Range

Lochcarron (1908)

Strathcarron, Ross-shire IV54 8YU
Tel: 01520 766211   Fax: 01520 766211
Green Fee: ①   9 Holes   3578 yds   SSS: 60
Visitors: Anyday   Designer: Unknown
Short seaside links course. Magnificent setting on the shoreland

Resipole (1997)

Acharacle, Argyllshire PH36 4HX
Tel: 01967 431235   Fax: 01967 431777
Green Fee: ①   18 Holes   3708 yds   SSS: 60
Visitors: Anyday   Designers: Various
Beautifully laid out along the shore of Loch Sunart

Skeabost (1982)

Skeabost Bridge, By Portree, Isle of Skye IV51 9NP
Tel: 01470 532202   Fax: 01470 532454
Green Fee: ①   9 Holes   3224 yds   SSS: 59
Visitors: Anyday   Designer: John Stuart
Parkland course in the grounds of the Skeabost Hotel

Spean Bridge (1951)

Station Road, Spean Bridge, Inverness-shire PH34 4EU
Tel: 01397 703907 or 704954
Green Fee: ①   9 Holes   4542 yds   SSS: 63
Visitors: Anyday   Designer: Unknown
Park/heathland course with fine views including Ben Nevis

Stornaway (1890)

Lady Lever Park, Stornaway, Isle of Lewis HS2 0XP
Tel: 01851 702240 or 703654
Green Fee: ①   18 Holes   5252 yds   SSS: 67
Visitors: Anyday (No Sunday play)   Designer: J. R. Strutt
Picturesque parkland course with pleasant views

Traigh (1995)

Arisaig, Inverness-shire PH39 4NT
Tel: 01687 450628 or 450337
Green Fee: ①   9 Holes   4810 yds   SSS: 65
Visitors: Anyday   Designer: John Salvesen
Links course with breathtaking sea views

Ullapool (1998)

Morefield, Ullapool, Ross-shire IV26 2TH
Tel: 01854 613323 or 612348   Fax: 01854 613133
Green Fee: ①   9 Holes   5338 yds   SSS: 66
Visitors: Anyday   Designer: Unknown
Picturesque seaside course on the outskirts of Ullapool which is a traditional fishing village

Stornoway

A859

Isle
of
Harris

Tarbert

A859

South
Harris

Idrigil

A

A850

Port

A8

Benbecula

Askernish

Barra

Run

E

Outer Hebrides

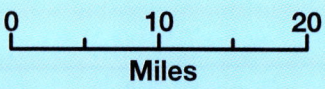

Inner Hebrides

| 0 | 10 | 20 |

Miles

Port of Ness

Durness

A838

A838

A894

A838

A837

le of
ewis

A835

A837

Ullapool

A832

A835

Gairloch

A832

A832

Achnasheen

A896

A890

A896

Lochcarron

keaboat

A890

Isle of
Skye

Kyle of
Lochalsh

A87

A87

A887

A82

ye

A87

A82

Maillaig

Spean
Bridge

Traigh

A830

A86

A861

Fort
William

Resipole

A82

Alness (1898)

Ardross Road, Alness, Ross-shire IV17 0QA
Tel: 01349 883877

Green Fee: ①   18 Holes   4886 yds   SSS: 64
Visitors: Anyday   Designer: John Sutherland
Fine views over Cromarty Firth, the course was extended in 1997 to 18 holes

Asta (1992)

Scalloway, Shetland Island ZE1 0UQ
Tel: 01595 880231
Green Fee: ①   9 Holes   5010 yds   SSS: 64
Visitors: Anyday   Designer: Jim Leask
Parkland course bordered by two lochs which come into play. Very scenic

Bonar Bridge / Ardgay (1904)

Market Stance, Migdale Rd, Bonar Bridge, Sutherland IV24 3EJ
Tel: 01863 766375 or 766119   Fax: 01863 766738

Green Fee: ①   9 Holes   5284 yds   SSS: 66
Visitors: Anyday   Designer: Unknown
Wooded moorland course with picturesque views of the Loch Migdale

Brora (1891)

43 Golf Road, Brora, Sutherland KW9 6QS
Tel: 01408 621417   Fax: 01408 622157
Green Fee: ②   18 Holes   6110 yds   SSS: 69
Visitors: Anyday   Designer: James Braid in 1923
Testing seaside links where in season there is gorse, juniper and thyme

The Carnegie Club (1994)

Skibo Castle, Dornoch, Sutherland IV25 3RQ
Tel: 01862 894600   Fax: 01862 894601   Pro: 01862 881260
Green Fee: ⑥   18 Holes   6671 yds   SSS: 72
Visitors: Weekdays   Designer: Donald Steel
Wonderful setting for this fine traditional links course

Golspie (1889)

Ferry Road, Golspie, Sutherland KW10 6ST
Tel: 01408 633266   Fax: 01408 633393

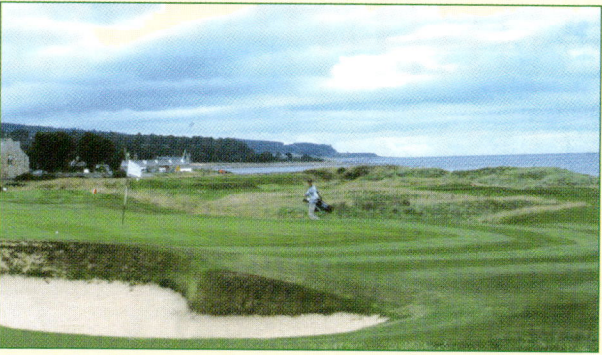

Green Fee: ②   18 Holes   5890 yds   SSS: 68
Visitors: Anyday   Designer: James Braid
Classic mixture of links, heathland and wonderful scenery

Helmsdale (1895)

The Strath, Helmsdale, Sutherland KW8 6JA
Tel: 01431 821063
Green Fee: ①   9 Holes   3720 yds   SSS: 61
Visitors: Anyday   Designer: Unknown
Short course with bracken, gorse and broom. Panoramic views

Invergordon (1893)

King George Street, Invergordon, Ross-shire IV18 0BD
Tel: 01349 852715   Fax: 01349 852715
Green Fee: ①   18 Holes   6030 yds   SSS: 69
Visitors: Anyday   Designers: A. Rae in1994/J. Urquhart
Parkland course situated alongside the waters of Cromarty Firth

Lybster (1926)

Main Street, Lybster, Caithness KW3 6AE
Tel: 01593 721201 or 721316
Green Fee: ①   9 Holes   3858 yds   SSS: 61
Visitors: Anyday   Designer: Unknown
Parkland with heather edged fairways

Orkney (1889)
Grainbank, Kirkwall, Orkney KW15 1RD
Tel: 01856 872457
Green Fee: ①   18 Holes   5411 yds   SSS: 67
Visitors: Anyday   Designer: Unknown
Open parkland course with marvellous views of Kirkwall

Reay (1893)
Reay, Thurso, Caithness KW14 7RE
Tel: 01847 811288   Fax: 01847 894189
Green Fee: ②   18 Holes   5831 yds   SSS: 69
Visitors: Anyday   Designer: Unknown
Seaside links course alongside Sandsie Bay with views over Pentland Firth and Orkney

Royal Dornoch (1877)
Golf Road, Dornoch, Sutherland IV25 3LW
Tel: 01862 810219   Fax: 01862 810792   Pro: 01862 810902

Green Fee: ④   Championship: 18 Holes   6514 yds   SSS: 73
          ②   Struie: 18 Holes   5438 yds   SSS: 69
Visitors: Anyday   Designers: Tom Morris/J. Sutherland/G. Duncan
One of Scotland's best links courses with gorse and broom

Sanday (1977)
Sanday, Orkney KW17 2BW
Tel: 01857 600341   Fax: 01857 600341
Green Fee: ①   9 Holes   5552 yds   SSS: 70
Visitors: Anyday   Designer: John Stark
Scenic views. Nature at its best. Pay one green fee to be a member for a year. Must be cheapest in Scotland

Shetland (1891)
Dale, Shetland Island ZE2 9SB
Tel: 01595 840369   Fax: 01595 840369
Green Fee: ①   18 Holes   5776 yds   SSS: 68
Visitors: Anyday   Designer: Fraser Middleton
Hilly and challenging moorland course

Stromness (1890)

Ness Road, Stromness, Orkney KW16 3DU
Tel: 01856 850772 or 850885

Green Fee: ①   18 Holes   4762 yds   SSS: 63
Visitors: Weekdays   Designer: George Smith

Testing parkland/seaside course with magnificent views of the Scapa Flow

Tain (1890)

Chapel Road, Tain, Ross-shire IV19 1JE
Tel: 01862 892314   Fax: 01862 892099   Pro: 01862 893313

Green Fee: ③   18 Holes   6404 yds   SSS: 71
Visitors: Anyday   Designer: Tom Morris

Beautiful sheltered course overlooking the Dornoch Firth

Tarbat (1909)

Tarbat Ness Road, Portmahomack, Ross-shire IV20 1YB
Tel: 01862 871598   Fax: 01862 871598

Green Fee: ①   9 Holes   5082 yds   SSS: 66
Visitors: Anyday   Designer: John Sutherland

Links course with spectacular views

Thurso (1893)

Newlands of Geise, Thurso, Caithness KW14 7XD
Tel: 01847 893807

Green Fee: ①   18 Holes   5853 yds   SSS: 69
Visitors: Anyday   Designer: W. Stuart

Lovely parkland course with panoramic views across to the Orkneys. Most northern mainland course

Whalsay (1975)

Skaw Taing, Isle of Whalsay, Shetland Islands ZE2 9AA
Tel: 01806 566705   Sec: 01806 566450

Green Fee: ①   18 Holes   6009 yds   SSS: 68
Visitors: Anyday   Designer: Unknown

Exposed moorland course with spectacular scenery and an abundance of wildlife. Most northern club in Britain

Wick (1870)

Reiss, By Wick, Caithness KW1 4RW
Tel: 01955 602726 or 602935

Green Fee: ②   18 Holes   6200 yds   SSS: 70
Visitors: Anyday   Designer: Sir George Dumbar

True links situated in natural beauty alongside Sinclair's Bay

Rea

A838

A836

A836

A897

B871

A836

B873

B871

A836

A838

A897

A836

Bre

A837

A839

A839

A9

Golspie

A837

B864

Bonar
Bridge &
Ardgay

Carngie
Club

A9

B9168

A836

Royal Dornoc

A949

A836

A949

Tain

Ta

B9176

B9174

A9

B9165

B9175

B9166

Alness

A9

Invergordon

B817

Cromarty

B817

A832

John O'Groats

B855

A836

Thurso

A836

A9

B874

B876

B870

B874

B876

B870

A99

Wick

B870

B870

B873

B870

A882

Wick

A9

A99

Lybster

A9

Helmsdale

S H E T L A N D

Unst

Yell

Fetlar

Whalsay

Asta

Shetland

Sanday

Rousay

Eday

Stronsay

Orkney

Shapinsay

Kirkwall

Stromness

O R K N E Y

HOY

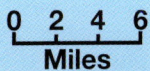

0 2 4 6

Miles

Area Three

Abernethy (1893)

Nethy Bridge, Inverness-shire PH25 3ED
Tel: 01479 821305   Fax: 01479 821196
Green Fee: ①   9 Holes   5038 yds   SSS: 66
Visitors: Anyday   Designer: Unknown
Undulating moorland course surrounded by majestic pine trees

Aigas (1993)

Mains of Aigas, By Beauly, Inverness-shire IV4 7AD
Tel: 01463 782942   Fax: 01463 782423
Green Fee: ①   9 Holes   4878 yds   SSS: 63
Visitors: Anyday   Designer: Bill Mitchell
Undulating parkland course with natural beauty and wildlife

Ballater (1892)

Victoria Road, Ballater, Aberdeenshire AB35 5QX
Tel: 01339 755567   Fax: 01339 755057   Pro: 01339 755658
Green Fee: ②   18 Holes   6112 yds   SSS: 69
Visitors: Anyday   Designer: James Braid
Charming and challenging moorland course

Blair Atholl (1896)

Invertilt Road, Blair Atholl, Perthshire PH18 5TG
Tel: 01796 481407 or 481274   Fax: 01796 481751
Green Fee: ①   9 Holes   5816 yds   SSS: 68
Visitors: Anyday   Designer: Tom Morris
Parkland course with river alongside three holes

Boat of Garten (1898)

Boat of Garten, Inverness-shire PH24 3BQ
Tel: 01479 831282   Fax: 01479 831523

Green Fee: ②   18 Holes   5866 yds   SSS: 69
Visitors: Anyday   Designer: James Braid
Wonderful undulating heathland course. Very popular, should not be missed

Braemar (1902)

Cluniebank Road, Braemar, Aberdeenshire AB35 5XX
Tel: 01339 741618 Fax: 01339 41400
Green Fee: ①   18 Holes   4935 yds   SSS: 64
Visitors: Anyday   Designer: Joe Anderson
Park/moorland course with River Clunie running through. Highest course in Scotland

Buckpool (1965)

Barhill Road, Buckie, Morayshire AB56 1DU
Tel: 01542 832236   Fax: 01542 832236

Green Fee: ①   18 Holes   6257 yds   SSS: 70
Visitors: Anyday   Designers: Hawtree & Taylor
Seaside links course enjoying fantastic views

Carrbridge (1980)

Inverness Road, Carrbridge, Inverness-shire PH23 3AU
Tel: 01479 841623 or 841506

Green Fee: ①   9 Holes   5402 yds   SSS: 68
Visitors: Anyday   Designer: Unknown
Set in beautiful scenery, the course is a mixture of parkland and heathland

Dalmunzie (1922)

Spittal of Glenshee, Blairgowrie, Perthshire PH10 7QG
Tel: 01250 885226 Fax: 01250 885225
Green Fee: ①   9 Holes   4198 yds   SSS: 61
Visitors: Anyday   Designer: Alister MacKenzie
Short and hilly highland parkland course. One of the highest in Scotland

Dufftown (1896)

Tomintoul Road, Dufftown, Keith, Morayshire AB55 4BS
Tel: 01340 820325   Fax: 01340 820325
Green Fee: ①   18 Holes   5308 yds   SSS: 67
Visitors: Anyday   Designer: A. Simpson
Superb scenery overlooking the town

Elgin (1906)

Hardhillock, Birnie Road, Elgin, Morayshire IV30 8SX
Tel: 01343 542338   Fax: 01343 542341   Pro: 01343 542884

Green Fee: ②   18 Holes   6411 yds   SSS: 71
Visitors: Anyday   Designer: John MacPherson
One of the finest parkland courses in Scotland

Forres (1889)

Muiryshade, Forres, Morayshire IV36 2RD
Tel: 01309 672949 Fax: 01309 672250 Pro: 01309 672250

Green Fee: ②   18 Holes   6236 yds   SSS: 70
Visitors: Anyday   Designers: James Braid/Willie Park
Parkland course in wooded countryside

Fort Augustus (1905)

Markethill, Fort Augustus, Inverness-shire PH32 4DP
Tel: 01320 366460 or 366309
Green Fee: ①   9 Holes   5454 yds   SSS: 67
Visitors: Anyday   Designer: Dr. Lane
Moorland course bordered by tree-lined Caledonian Canal

Fortrose & Rosemarkie (1888)

Ness Road East, Fortrose, Ross-shire IV10 8SE
Tel: 01381 620529   Fax: 01381 621328
Green Fee: ②   18 Holes   5883 yds   SSS: 69
Visitors: Anyday   Designer: James Braid
Superb links course almost surrounded by the sea

Garmouth & Kingston (1932)

Garmouth, Fochabers, Morayshire IV32 7NJ
Tel: 01343 870388   Fax: 01343 870388
Green Fee: ①   18 Holes   5935 yds   SSS: 69
Visitors: Anyday   Designer: George Smith
Seaside course on the banks of the River Spey

Grantown-on-Spey (1890)

Golf Course Road, Grantown-on-Spey, Morayshire PH26 3HY
Tel: 01479 872079   Fax: 01479 873725

Green Fee: ②   18 Holes   5710 yds   SSS: 68
Visitors: Anyday   Designer: Willie Park
Parkland and woodland course with magnificent views

Hopeman (1923)

Hopeman, Morayshire IV30 5YA
Tel: 01343 830578   Fax: 01343 815102

Green Fee: ①   18 Holes   5590 yds   SSS: 67
Visitors: Anyday   Designer: J. MacKenzie
Seaside links type course with views of Moray Firth

Inverness (1883)

Culcabock Road, Inverness IV2 3XQ
Tel: 01463 239882 Fax: 01463 239882 Pro: 01463 231989

Green Fee: ③   18 Holes   6256 yds   SSS: 70
Visitors: Anyday   Designer: Unknown
Parkland course with many trees and burn running through

Keith (1963)

Fife Park, Keith, Morayshire AB55 5DY
Tel: 01542 882469   Fax: 01542 888176

Green Fee: ①   18 Holes   5802 yds   SSS: 68
Visitors: Anyday   Designer: Unknown
Undulating parkland course with panoramic views

Kingussie (1891)

Gynack Road, Kingussie, Inverness-shire PH21 1LR
Tel: 01540 661600   Fax: 01540 662066
Green Fee: ②   18 Holes   5615 yds   SSS: 68
Visitors: Anyday   Designer: Harry Vardon
Rolling parkland course with stunning views

Kinloss (1997)

Kinloss, Forres, Morayshire IV36 2UB
Tel: 01343 850585   Fax: 01343 850242
Green Fee: ①   18 Holes   5474 yds   SSS: 68
Visitors: Anyday   Designer: Green Staff Services
Parkland course with views of Moray Firth

Loch Ness (1996)

Castle Heather, Inverness, Inverness-shire IV2 6AA
Tel: 01463 713335   Fax: 01463 712695   Pro: 01463 713334
Green Fee: ②   18 Holes   6722 yds   SSS: 72
Visitors: Anyday   Designer: Caddies
Parkland course with fine views

Moray (1889)

Stotfield Road, Lossiemouth, Morayshire IV31 6QS
Tel: 01343 812018   Fax: 01343 815102

Green Fee: ③ Old   18 Holes   6617 yds   SSS: 73
Green Fee: ② New   18 Holes   6005 yds   SSS: 69
Visitors: Anyday   Designers: Tom Morris (Old) Sir Henry Cotton (New)
Excellent links courses with superb views

Muir of Ord (1875)

Great North Road, Muir of Ord, Ross-shire IV6 7SX
Tel: 01463 870825   Fax: 01463 871867

Green Fee: ①   18 Holes   5596 yds   SSS: 68
Visitors: Anyday   Designer: James Braid (Part)
Heathland course with a road and railway line running through

Nairn (1887)

Seabank Road, Nairn, Inverness-shire IV12 4HB
Tel: 01667 453208   Fax: 01667 456328   Pro: 01667 452787

Green Fee: ⑤   18 Holes   6430 yds   SSS: 73
Visitors: Anyday   Designers: A. Simpson/T. Morris/J. Braid
One of the best traditional Scottish links created from a wilderness of whims and heather. Not to be missed

Nairn Dunbar (1899)

Lochloy Road, Nairn, Inverness-shire IV12 5AE
Tel: 01667 452741   Fax: 01667 456897
Green Fee: ③   18 Holes   6720 yds   SSS: 73
Visitors: Anyday   Designer: Unknown
Seaside links type course where gorse and whims abound

Newtonmore (1893)

Golf Course Road, Newtonmore, Inverness-shire PH20 1AT
Tel: 01540 673328   Fax: 01540 673878   Pro: 01540 673611
Green Fee: ①   18 Holes   6041 yds   SSS: 69
Visitors: Anyday   Designer: James Braid
Moorland/parkland course

Pitlochry (1908)

Golf Course Road, Pitlochry, Perthshire PH16 5QY
Tel: 01796 472792   Fax: 01796 473599
Green Fee: ②   18 Holes   5811 yds   SSS: 69
Visitors: Anyday   Designers: W. Fernie/Major C. Hutchinson
A heathland course with fine views. Interesting and varied

Rothes (1990)

Blackhall, Rothes, Morayshire AB38 7AN
Tel: 01340 831443 or 831277   Fax: 01340 831443
Green Fee: ①   9 Holes   4972 yds   SSS: 64
Visitors: Anyday   Designer: John Souter
Moorland course partly surrounded by pine forest

Spey Bay (1906)

Spey Bay, Fochabers, Morayshire IV32 7PJ
Tel: 01343 820424   Fax: 01343 829282
Green Fee: ②   18 Holes   6092 yds   SSS: 69
Visitors: Anyday   Designer: Ben Sayers
Undulating seaside links course with superb views

Strathlene (1877)

Portessie, Buckie, Banffshire AB56 2DJ
Tel: 01542 831798 or 832236   Fax: 01542 831798
Green Fee: ①   18 Holes   5977 yds   SSS: 69
Visitors: Anyday   Designer: George Smith
Undulating seaside course with unsurpassed views over the Moray Firth

Strathpeffer Spa (1888)

Golf Course Road, Strathpeffer, Ross-shire IV14 9AS
Tel: 01997 421219   Fax: 01997 421011   Pro: 01997 421011

Green Fee: ①   18 Holes   4792 yds   SSS: 64
Visitors: Anyday   Designer: Tom Morris
Upland course with natural hazards and panoramic views. Extremely scenic

Torvean (1962)

Glenurquhart Road, Inverness, Inverness-shire IV3 8JN
Tel: 01463 711434 or 225651   Fax: 01463 225651

Green Fee: ①   18 Holes   5784 yds   SSS: 68
Visitors: Anyday   Designer: T. Hamilton
Flat parkland course alongside the Caledonian Canal

Miles

0 2 4 6

A887

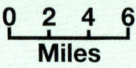

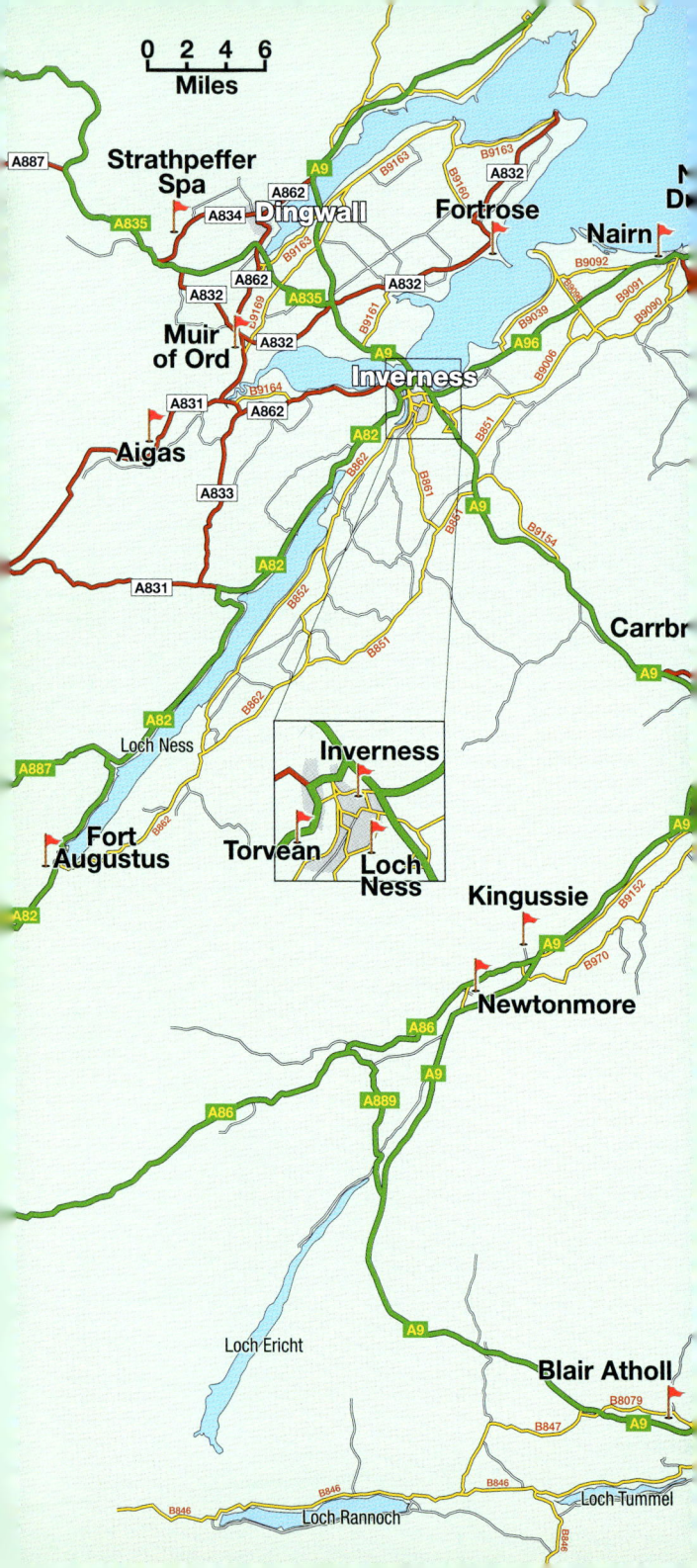

Strathpeffer Spa

A835

A834

A862

Dingwall

B9163

B9163

B9160

A832

Fortrose

Nairn

B9092

B9091

B9090

B9039

A96

B9006

A835

A832

A862

B9169

A832

Muir of Ord

A831

B9164

A862

Aigas

A833

Inverness

A9

A82

B862

B861

B851

A9

B9154

A831

A82

B852

B851

Carrbr

A9

B862

A82

Loch Ness

A887

B862

Inverness

Fort Augustus

Torvean

Loch Ness

A82

Kingussie

A9

B9152

B970

A9

A86

Newtonmore

A9

A86

A889

A9

Loch Ericht

Blair Atholl

B8079

B847

A9

B846

B846

Loch Rannoch

B846

Loch Tummel

Area 3

Hopeman Moray Strathlene
Garmouth
Kinloss Elgin Spey Bay Buckpool
Buckie
Forres Elgin Keith Keith
Rothes
Dufftown Dufftown
Grantown
Grantown-on-Spey
Abernethy
Boat of Garten
Ballater
Braemar
Dalmunzie

A96 B9012 B9013 B9069 B9010 A941 B9103 B9015 B9103 B9017 A95
A98 B9014 A96 B9016 A95 B9014 A96 B9115 B9012 A95 B9009 B9008
A939 A940 B9007 A938 B970 B9138 B9008 B9002 A97 A97 A944 A97
A939 A939 A939 B976 B976 A93 B976 A97 B9119 A93
A93 A93 B955 B955 A924 B951 B950 A924 A93 B951 B957 B9119 A9

Area Four

Aboyne (1881)

Formaston Park, Aboyne, Aberdeenshire AB34 5HP
Tel: 013398 86328   Fax: 013398 87592   Pro: 013398 86469
Green Fee: ②   18 Holes   5975 yds   SSS: 69
Visitors: Anyday   Designer: Unknown
Beautiful part parkland, part heathland course situated by two lochs

Alford (1982)

Montgarrie Road, Alford, Aberdeenshire AB33 8AE
Tel: 01975 562178   Fax: 01975 562178
Green Fee: ①   18 Holes   5483 yds   SSS: 66
Visitors: Anyday   Designer: David Hurd
Parkland course with road, railway and burn running through

Auchmill (1975)

Bonnyview Road, Auchmill, Aberdeenshire AB2 7FQ
Tel: 01224 693312 or 715214   Fax: 01224 715226
Green Fee: ①   18 Holes   5883 yds   SSS: 68
Visitors: Anyday   Designer: Neil Coles/Brian Hugget
Pay and play parkland difficult tree-lined course

Balnagask (1955)

St Fitticks Road, Balnagask, Aberdeenshire AB1 3QT
Tel: 01224 876407 or 871286   Pro: 01224 648693
Green Fee: ①   18 Holes   6065 yds   SSS: 69
Visitors: Anyday   Designer: Hawtree & Son
Pay and play seaside course. Very undulating

Banchory (1905)

Kinneskie Road, Banchory, Aberdeenshire AB31 5TA
Tel: 01330 822365   Fax: 01330 822491   Pro: 01330 822447

Green Fee: ②   18 Holes   5781 yds   SSS: 68
Visitors: Anyday   Designer: John Souter
Parkland course by River Dee. Woodland scenery

Craibstone (1998)

Craibstone Estate, Bucksburn, Aberdeenshire AB21 9YA
Tel: 01224 716777   Fax: 01224 711298

Green Fee: ①   18 Holes   5613 yds   SSS: 69
Visitors: Anyday   Designer: Greens of Scotland
Parkland/woodland course with pleasant views

Cruden Bay (1899)

Aulton Road, Cruden Bay, Aberdeenshire AB42 0NN
Tel: 01779 812285   Fax: 01779 812945   Pro: 01779 812414

Green Fee: ④   Cruden   18 Holes   6395 yds   SSS: 72
                    St. Olaf   9 Holes   5106 yds   SSS: 64
Visitors: Weekdays   Designer: Thomas Simpson
Wonderful seaside links course of the highest order. Magnificent views. Not to be missed

Cullen (1879)

The Links, Cullen, Buckie, Banffshire AB56 4WB
Tel: 01542 840685   Sec: 01542 840174   Fax: 01542 841977
Green Fee: ①   18 Holes   4610 yds   SSS: 62
Visitors: Anyday   Designer: Tom Morris
Interesting seaside course with wonderful scenery

Deeside (1903)

Golf Road, Bieldside, Aberdeen, Aberdeenshire AB15 9DL
Tel: 01224 869457   Fax: 01224 869457   Pro: 01224 861041
Green Fee: ③   18 Holes   6286 yds   SSS: 71
                    ②   18 Holes   5581 yds   SSS: 67
Visitors: Anyday   Designer: Unknown
Parkland course alongside river, also has 9 hole course

Duff House Royal (1909)

The Banyards, Banff, Banffshire AB45 3SX
Tel: 01261 812062   Fax: 01261 812224   Pro: 01261 812075
Green Fee: ②   18 Holes   6161 yds   SSS: 70
Visitors: Anyday   Designer: Dr. Alister McKenzie
Well kept parkland course with large two-tier greens

Dunecht House (1925)

Dunecht, Skene, Aberdeenshire AB32 7AW
Tel: 01330 860223 Fax: 01330 860325

Green Fee: ①   9 Holes   6270 yds   SSS: 70
Visitors: Members, Guests   Designer: Unknown
Wooded parkland course

East Aberdeenshire (1999)

Millden, Balmedie, Aberdeenshire AB23 8YY
Tel: 01358 742111   Fax: 01358 742123
Green Fee: ①   18 Holes   6276 yds   SSS: 71
Visitors: Anyday   Designer: Ian Creswell
New course with young trees and views of the North Sea and Aberdeen City

Fraserburgh (1882)

Philorth, Fraserburgh, Aberdeenshire AB43 8TL
Tel: 01346 516616   Fax: 01346 516616   Tel: 01346 517898
Green Fee: ①   Corbie   18 Holes   6278 yds   SSS: 70
            ①   Rosehill   9 Holes   4810 yds   SSS: 64
Visitors: Weekdays   Designer: James Braid
Undulating seaside course. Very scenic

Hazelhead (1927)

Hazelhead Park, Aberdeen, Aberdeenshire AB15 8BD
Tel: 01224 310711 or 321830   Fax: 01224 648693
Green Fee: ①   No. 1   18 Holes   6211 yds   SSS: 70
            ①   No. 2   18 Holes   5742 yds   SSS: 68
Visitors: Anyday   Designer: Dr. Alistair MacKenize
Two pay and play moorland courses, also has a 9 hole course

Huntly (1892)

Cooper Park, Huntly, Aberdeenshire AB54 4SH
Tel: 01466 792643   Fax: 01466 792360   Pro: 01466 794023
Green Fee: ①   18 Holes   5399 yds   SSS: 66
Visitors: Anyday   Designer: Unknown
Parkland course lying between Rivers Deveron and Bogie

Inchmarlo (1995)
Glassel Road, Inchmarlo, Banchory, Aberdeenshire AB31 4BQ
Tel: 01330 822557   Fax: 01330 822557
Green Fee: (3)   Lairds   18 Holes   6218 yds   SSS: 71
         (1)   No. 2   9 Holes   4300 yds   SSS: 62
Visitors: Anyday   Designer: Graeme Webster
Pay and play parkland course with many mature trees. Gently sloping

Insch (1997)
Golf Terrace, Insch, Aberdeenshire AB52 6JY
Tel: 01464 820363   Fax: 01464 820363
Green Fee: (1)   18 Holes   5350 yds   SSS: 67
Visitors: Anyday   Designer: Greens of Scotland
Undulating parkland course with panoramic views

Area 4

Inverallochy (1888)
Cairnbulg, Inverallochy, Aberdeenshire AB43 8XY
Tel: 01346 582000   Sec: 01346 582096
Green Fee: (1)   18 Holes   5244 yds   SSS: 66
Visitors: Anyday   Designer: Unknown
Pay and play typical seaside links

Inverurie (1923)
Blackhall Road, Inverurie, Aberdeenshire AB51 5JB
Tel: 01467 624080   Fax: 01467 621051   Pro: 01467 620193
Green Fee: (1)   18 Holes   5711 yds   SSS: 68
Visitors: Anyday   Designer: G. Smith and J. M. Stutt
Parkland course. Part enclosed, part through wooded area

Kemnay (1908)
Monymusk Road, Kemnay, Aberdeenshire AB51 5RA
Tel: 01467 643746   Fax: 01467 643746   Tel: 01467 642225

Green Fee: (1)   18 Holes   6342 yds   SSS: 69
Visitors: Anyday   Designer: Greens of Scotland
Undulating parkland course with marvellous views

Kings Links (1873)
Aberdeen, Aberdeenshire AB24 5QB
Tel: 01224 632269   Fax: 01224 648693
Green Fee: (1)   18 Holes   6270 yds   SSS: 70
Visitors: Anyday   Designer: Unknown
Pay and play seaside links course with lots of bunkers

Kintore (1911)

Balbithan Road, Kintore, Aberdeenshire AB51 0UR
Tel: 01467 632631   Fax: 01467 632995
Green Fee: (1)   18 Holes   6019 yds   SSS: 69
Visitors: Anyday   Designer: Unknown
Undulating moorland course

Longside (1971)

Main St. Longside, Peterhead, Aberdeenshire AB42 4XJ
Tel: 01779 821558   Fax: 01779 821564

Green Fee: (1)   18 Holes   5225 yds   SSS: 66
Visitors: Anyday   Designer: Local Residents
Parkland course with the Ugie River in play on many holes

Lumphanan (1994)

10 Main Road, Lumphanan, Aberdeenshire AB31 4PX
Tel: 01339 883589 or 883480

Green Fee: (1)   9 Holes   3718 yds   SSS: 62
Visitors: Anyday   Designer: Greens of Scotland
Hillside course with outstanding views of Royal Deeside

McDonald (1927)

Hospital Road, Ellon, Aberdeenshire AB41 9AW
Tel: 01358 720576 Fax: 01358 720001 Pro: 01358 722891
Green Fee: ① 18 Holes 5991 yds SSS: 70
Visitors: Anyday Designer: Unknown
Tight parkland course with streams running through

Meldrum House (1998)

Meldrum Estate, Old Meldrum, Aberdeenshire AB51 0AE
Tel: 01651 873553 Fax: 01651 873635
Green Fee: ① 18 Holes 6470 yds SSS: 72
Visitors: Hotel Guests Designer: Graeme Webster
Parkland course with water in play at 8 holes

Murcar (1909)

Bridge of Don, Aberdeen, Aberdeenshire AB23 8BD
Tel: 01224 704354 Fax: 01224 704354 Pro: 01224 704370

Green Fee: ③ Murcar 18 Holes 6287 yds SSS: 71
         ① Strabathie 9 Holes 5392 yds SSS: 67
Visitors: Anyday Designer: Archie Simpson
Traditional Scottish links course set among towering sand dunes

Newburgh-on-Ythan (1888)

Newburgh, Ellon, Aberdeenshire AB41 6BY
Tel: 01358 789438 or 789084
Green Fee: ① 18 Holes 6162 yds SSS: 71
Visitors: Anyday Designer: Unknown
Undulating seaside links course

Newmachar (1990)

Swailend, Newmachar, Aberdeenshire AB21 7UU
Tel: 01651 863002 Fax: 01651 863055 Tel: 01651 862127
Green Fee: ③ Hawkshill 18 Holes 6623 yds SSS: 74
         ① Swailend 18 Holes 6388 yds SSS: 71
Visitors: Anyday Designer: Dave Thomas
Parkland course with several lakes

Oldmeldrum (1885)

Kirk Brae, Oldmeldrum, Aberdeenshire AB51 0DJ
Tel: 01651 872648 Fax: 01651 873555 Pro: 01651 873555
Green Fee: ① 18 Holes 5988 yds SSS: 69
Visitors: Anyday Designer: Unknown
Superb views from this tree-lined parkland course

Peterculter (1989)

Burnside Road, Peterculter, Aberdeenshire AB51 0LN
Tel: 01224 735245   Fax: 01224 735580   Pro: 01224 734994
Green Fee: ①   18 Holes   5947 yds   SSS: 69
Visitors: Anyday   Designer: Greens of Scotland
Undulating scenic parkland course alongside the River Dee

Peterhead (1841)

Craigewan Links, Peterhead, Aberdeenshire AB42 6LT
Tel: 01779 472149   Fax: 01779 480725
Green Fee: ② Old   18 Holes   6173 yds   SSS: 71
        ① New   9 Holes   4474 yds   SSS: 62
Visitors: Anyday   Designer: Willie Park / James Braid
Testing natural links course bounded by the sea and River Ugie

Portlethen (1983)

Badentoy Road, Portlethen, Aberdeenshire AB12 4YA
Tel: 01224 781090   Fax: 01224 781090   Pro: 01224 782571

Green Fee: ①   18 Holes   6670 yds   SSS: 72
Visitors: Anyday   Designer: Donald Steel
Pleasant parkland course with mature trees & views of the North Sea

Rosehearty (1887)

1 Castle Street, Rosehearty, Aberdeenshire AB43 7JJ
Tel: 01346 571250   Fax: 01346 571306
Green Fee: ①   9 Holes   4394 yds   SSS: 62
Visitors: Anyday   Designer: Bob Strachan in 1974
Links course with fine views of Castle and North Sea

Royal Aberdeen (1780)

Balgownie, Bridge of Don, Aberdeenshire AB23 8AT
Tel: 01224 702571   Fax: 01224 826591   Pro: 01224 702221
Green Fee: ④ Balgownie   18 Holes   6415 yds   SSS: 73
        ① Silverburn   9 Holes   4021 yds   SSS: 61
Visitors: Anyday   Designer: Robert Simpson / James Braid
Championship seaside links. Sixth oldest golf club in the world

Royal Tarlair (1923)

Buchan Street, Macduff, Aberdeenshire AB44 1TA
Tel: 01261 832897   Fax: 01261 833455
Green Fee: ①   18 Holes   5866 yds   SSS: 68
Visitors: Anyday   Designer: George Smith
Seaside clifftop course

Tarland (1908)

Aberdeen Road, Tarland, Aberdeenshire AB34 4TB
Tel: 01339 881000   Fax: 01339 881000   Sec: 01339 881967
Green Fee: ①   9 Holes   5875 yds   SSS: 67
Visitors: Anyday   Designer: Tom Morris
Difficult upland parkland course but easy walking, magnificent scenery

Torphins (1896)

Bog Road, Torphins, Banchory, Aberdeenshire AB31 4JU
Tel: 01339 882115   Fax: 01339 882402
Green Fee: ①   9 Holes   4738 yds   SSS: 64
Visitors: Anyday   Designer: Unknown
Heathland course with fine views of the Cairngorns

Area 4

Turiff (1896)

Rosehall, Turriff, Aberdeenshire AB53 4HD
Tel: 01888 562982   Fax: 01888 568050   Pro: 01888 563025

Green Fee: ①   18 Holes   6145 yds   SSS: 69
Visitors: Anyday   Designer: G. M. Fraser
Picturesque parkland course alongside the River Deveron

Westhill (1977)

Westhill Heights, Skene, Aberdeenshire AB32 6RY
Tel: 01224 742567   Fax: 01224 749124   Pro: 01224 749124

Green Fee: ①   18 Holes   5849 yds   SSS: 69
Visitors: Anyday   Designer: Charles Lawrie
Undulating moorland / parkland course

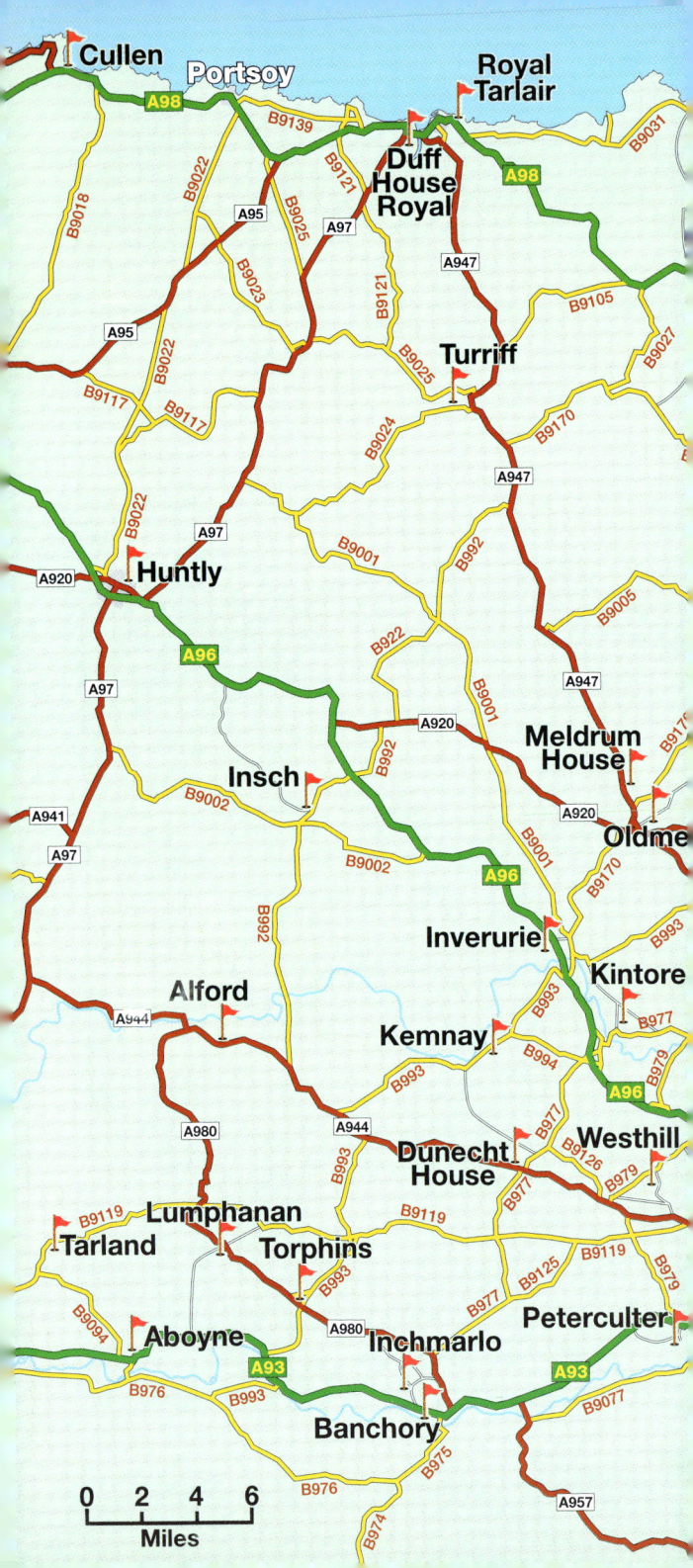

Cullen
Portsoy
Royal Tarlair
Duff House Royal
Turriff
Huntly
Insch
Meldrum House
Oldme
Inverurie
Kintore
Alford
Kemnay
Westhill
Dunecht House
Lumphanan
Tarland
Torphins
Peterculter
Aboyne
Inchmarlo
Banchory

A98
B9139
B9121
B9022
A95
B9025
A97
B9121
B9018
B9023
A947
B9105
B9031
B9027
A95
B9022
B9025
A947
B9117
B9117
B9024
B9170
A97
B9001
B992
A947
A920
A96
B922
B9005
A97
A920
B992
B9001
A941
B9002
B9002
A96
B9170
B992
B9001
A97
B9001
B993
A944
B993
B977
A96
B993
B994
B979
A980
A944
B993
B977
B9126
B979
B9119
B977
B9119
B9119
B9094
B9125
B977
B979
A980
A93
A93
B976
B993
B9077
B975
A957
B974
B976

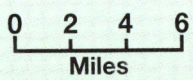

0 2 4 6
Miles

ehearty

Fraserburgh

Inverallochy

B9031

B9032

A90

B9033

A98

A981

B9093

A90

B9093

A952

A950

B9106 B9029

A981 A950

B9030

A90

Longside

Peterhead

A950

A952

A948

B9005

A90

McDonald

A90

Cruden Bay

A975

A920

B9000

Newburgh
-on-Ythan

B999

A90

vmachar

East Aberdeenshire

B977

B977

B977

Murcar

B997

stone

Aberdeen

B119

nethen

A90

Stoneywood

A90(T)

A947

Danestone

B999

Bridge of Don

Royal
Aberdeen

Auchmill

Nerthfield

Hilten

Coll

Kings
Links

Mastrick

Cornhill

A958

Summerhill

B9119

Mon

Hazelhead

Ferryhill

Balnagask

Braeside

Kaimhill

Tullos

Cults

A93

Deeside

Waterside

Alterns

Craighead

A90(T)

A956

Cove Bay

Alyth (1894)

Pitcrocknie, Alyth, Perthshire PH11 8HF
Tel: 01828 632268   Fax: 01828 633491   Pro: 01828 632411
Green Fee: ②   18 Holes   6205 yds   SSS: 71
Visitors: Anyday   Designer: James Braid
Excellent heathland course with roller coaster greens & panoramic views

Arbroath (1905)

Elliot, Arbroath, Angus DD11 2PE
Tel: 01241 872069 Fax: 01241 875837 Pro: 01241 875837

Green Fee: ①   18 Holes   6185 yds   SSS: 70
Visitors: Anyday   Designer: James Braid
Pay and play seaside course with the Dowrie burn in play

Auchenblae (1894)

Auchenblae, Laurencekirk, Kincardineshire AB30 1BU
Tel: 01561 320331 or 320002

Green Fee: ①   9 Holes   4452 yds   SSS: 64
Visitors: Anyday   Designer: Unknown
Pay and play picturesque parkland course with good views

Ballumbie Castle (2000)

3 Old Quarry Road, Dundee DD4 0SY
Tel: 01382 770028 Fax: 01382 730008

Green Fee: ① 18 Holes 6127 yds SSS: 70
Visitors: Anyday Designer: Duncan Gray
Tight parkland course with water hazards

Blairgowrie (1889)

Rosemount, Blairgowrie, Perthshire PH10 6LG
Tel: 01250 872622 Fax: 01250 872451 Pro: 01250 873116

Green Fee: ④ Rosemount 18 Holes 6588 yds SSS: 73
      ③ Lansdowne 18 Holes 6895 yds SSS: 73

Visitors: Weekdays

Designers: James Braid (Rosemount)
      P. Allis/D.Thomas (Lansdowne) 1974

Two excellent heathland courses with pine, heather, birch and broom in abundance

Brechin (1893)

Trinity, By Brechin, Angus DD9 7PD
Tel: 01356 622383   Fax: 01356 626295   Pro: 01356 625270

Green Fee: ①   18 Holes   6121 yds   SSS: 70
Visitors: Anyday   Designer: James Braid
Rolling parkland course with magnificent views of the Grampians

Caird Park (1926)

Mains Loan, Dundee, Tayside DD4 9BX
Tel: 01382 438871   Fax: 01382 434601   Pro: 01382 459438
Green Fee: ①   18 Holes   6303 yds   SSS: 70
Visitors: Anyday   Designer: Unknown
Pay and play parkland course with Gelly burn running through

Camperdown Park (1959)

Camperdown Park, Dundee, Tayside DD2 4TF
Tel: 01382 432688 Fax: 01382 433211

Green Fee: ①   18 Holes   6561 yds   SSS: 72
Visitors: Anyday   Designer: Eric Brown
Beautiful pay and play parkland course with mature trees surrounding the imposing Camperdown House

Carnoustie (16th century)

Links Parade, Carnoustie, Angus DD7 7JE
Tel: 01241 853789   Fax: 01241 852720

Green Fee:	⑤	Championship	18 Holes	6941 yds	SSS: 75
1914	②	Burnside	18 Holes	6020 yds	SSS: 69
1981	②	Budden Links	18 Holes	5420 yds	SSS: 66

Visitors: Anyday

Designers: A. Robertson / Tom Morris / James Braid

Championship links golf at its finest and toughest as the Open 1999 proved. The Barry Burn comes into play on all the courses

Downfield (1932)

Turnberry Avenue, Dundee, Angus DD2 3QP
Tel: 01382 825595   Fax: 01382 813111   Pro: 01382 889246
Green Fee: ③   18 Holes   6803 yds   SSS: 73
Visitors: Anyday   Designer: C. K. Cotton
This undulating parkland is one of Scotland's finest and is used for Open qualifying.

Edzell (1895)

High St, Edzell, By Brechin, Angus DD9 7TF
Tel: 01356 647283   Fax: 01356 648094   Pro: 01356 648462
Green Fee: ② Old   18 Holes   6348 yds   SSS: 71
         ① West Water 9 Holes   4114 yds   SSS: 60
Visitors: Anyday   Designer: Bob Simpson
Moorland/parkland course at the foothills of the Grampian Mountains

Forfar (1871)

Cunninghill, Arbroath Road, Forfar, Angus DD8 2RL
Tel: 01307 463773   Fax: 01307 468495   Pro: 01307 465683
Green Fee: ②   18 Holes   6052 yds   SSS: 70
Visitors: Anyday   Designer: James Braid/Tom Morris
Undulating parkland course with pleasant views

Glenisla (1998)

Pitcrocknie, Alyth, Perthshire PH11 8JJ
Tel: 01828 632445 Fax: 01828 633749

Green Fee: (2)   18 Holes   6402 yds   SSS: 71
Visitors: Anyday   Designer: Anthony Wardle

Challenging parkland course with natural contours and pleasant views

Kirriemuir (1908)

Northmuir, Kirriemuir, Angus DD8 4LN
Tel: 01575 573317 Fax: 01575 574608 Pro: 01575 573317

Green Fee: (2)   18 Holes   5510 yds   SSS: 67
Visitors: Anyday   Designer: James Braid

Heathland course with Broom and tree-lined fairways. Beautiful views of surrounding countryside

Letham Grange (1985)

Letham Grange, Colliston, By Arbroath, Angus DD11 4RL
Tel: 01241 890373 Fax: 01241 890725 Pro: 01241 890377

Green Fee: (3)   Old   18 Holes   6968 yds   SSS: 73
             (1)   New   18 Holes   5528 yds   SSS: 68
Visitors: Anyday   Designer: Donald Steel/G. K. Smith

Old course is set in wooded estate with lochs and burns and tougher than the New

Monifieth (1850)

Princes St, Monifieth, Dundee, Angus DD5 4AW
Tel: 01382 532767 Fax: 01382 535553 Pro: 01382 532945

Green Fee: (3)   Medal   18 Holes   6657 yds   SSS: 72
             (1)   Ashludie   18 Holes   5123 yds   SSS: 66
Visitors: Anyday   Designer: James Braid

Natural seaside links

Montrose (1562)

Trail Drive, Montrose, Angus DD10 8SW
Tel: 01674 672932   Fax: 01674 671800   Pro: 01674 672634
Green Fee: ③   Medal   18 Holes   6496 yds   SSS: 72
           ①   Broomfield   18 Holes   4800 yds   SSS: 63
Visitors: Anyday   Designer: Willie Park in 1903
The 5th oldest club in the world. True links with undulating fairways and normally fast greens

Panmure (1845)

Burnside Road, Barry, Angus DD7 7RT
Tel: 01241 855120   Fax: 01241 859737   Pro: 01241 852460

Area 5

Green Fee: ③   18 Holes   6317 yds   SSS: 71
Visitors: Anyday   Designer: Unknown
*Tight gorse/pine-bordered fairways with rolling greens
makes this heath/links course quite demanding*

Piperdam (1998)

Fowlis, By Dundee, Angus DD2 5LP
Tel: 01382 581374   Fax: 01382 581102
Green Fee: ②   18 Holes   6025 yds   SSS: 72
Visitors: Anyday   Designer: Unknown
Pay and play parkland course with mature trees. Pleasant views of Piperdam

Stonehaven (1888)

Cowie, Stonehaven, Aberdeenshire AB39 3RH
Tel: 01569 762124   Fax: 01569 765973
Green Fee: ①   18 Holes   5103 yds   SSS: 66
Visitors: Anyday   Designer: A. Simpson
Challenging seaside course with pleasant views

Strathmore (1996)

Leroch, Alyth, Perthshire PH11 8NZ
Tel: 01828 633322   Fax: 01828 633533
Green Fee: ②   Rannaleroch 18 Holes   6454 yds   SSS: 72
           ①   Leitfie   9 Holes   3438 yds   SSS: 58
Visitors: Anyday   Designer: John Salvesen
Pay and play hilly parkland course with fabulous views

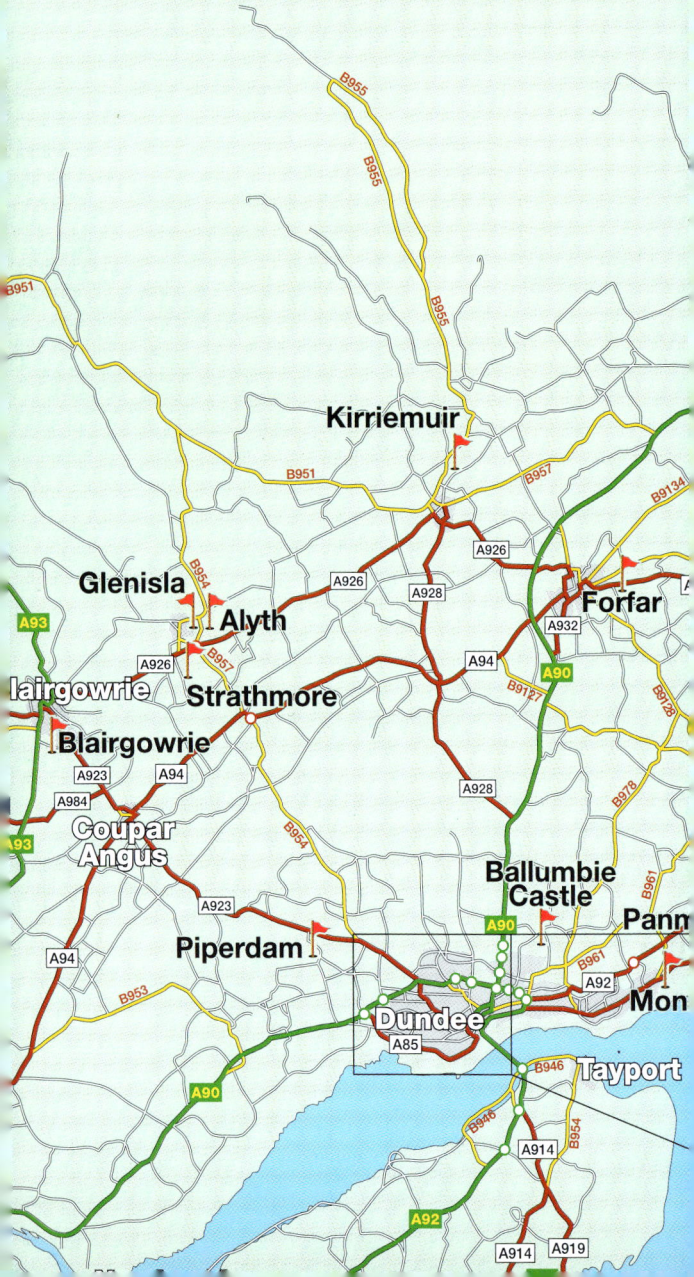

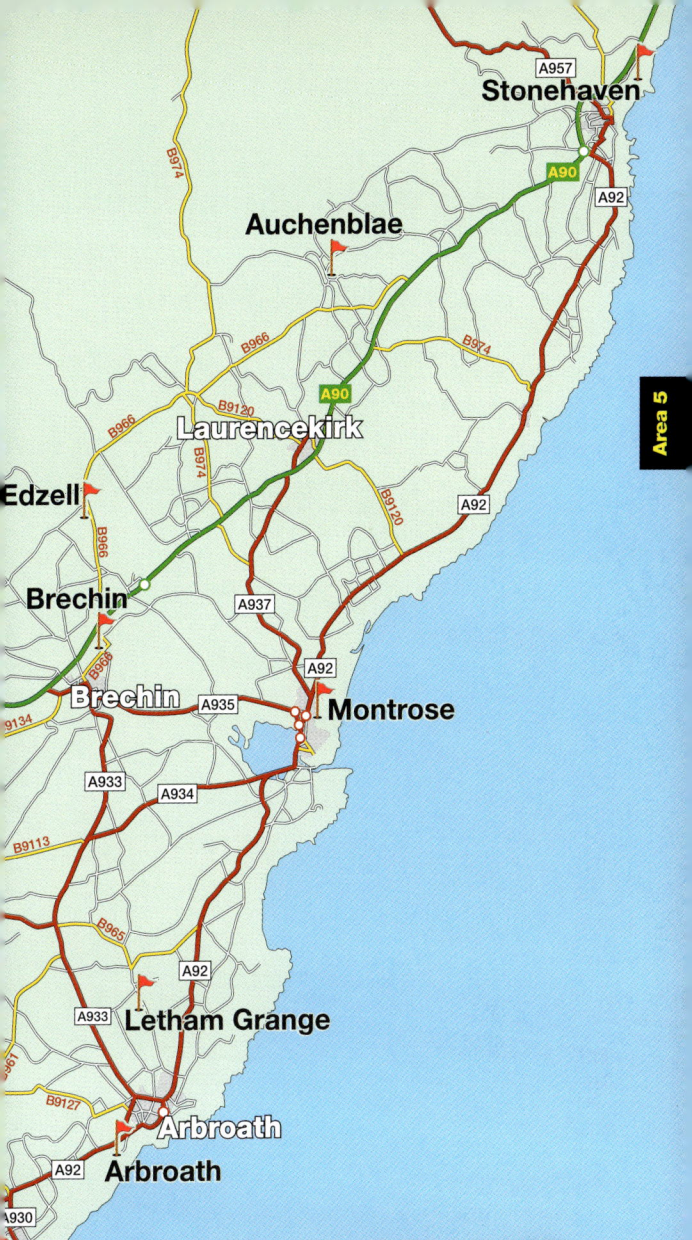

Stonehaven
A957
A90
A92

Auchenblae

Area 5

A90

Laurencekirk
B9120
B966
B974

Edzell
B966

A92

Brechin
Brechin
A937
A935
A933
A934
A92
Montrose

B9113
B965

Letham Grange
A92
A933

B9127
Arbroath
Arbroath
A92
A930

Carnoustie

Downfield
A90
Camperdown Park
Caird Park
A90
A923
A92
A85

Carradale (1906)

Carradale, Campbeltown, Argyllshire PA28 6QT
Tel: 01583 431378
Green Fee: ① 9 Holes 4784 yds SSS: 64
Visitors: Anyday Designer: Unknown
Difficult but scenic course with sea views

Colonsay (1880)

Isle of Colonsay, Argyllshire PA61 7YP
Tel: 01951 200364 or 200316 Fax: 01951 200312
Green Fee: ① 18 Holes 4775 yds SSS: 64
Visitors: Anyday Designer: Unknown
Primitive but challenging course played on Hebridean machair

Craignure (1895)

Scallastle, Craignure, Isle of Mull PA64 5AP
Tel: 01680 300402 Fax: 01680 300402

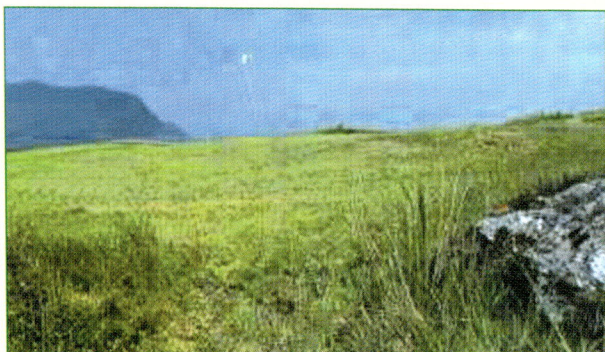

Green Fee: ① 9 Holes 5351 yds SSS: 66
Visitors: Anyday Designer: Unknown
Natural links course overlooking the Sound of Mull

Dalmally (1986)

Old Saw Mill, Dalmally, Argyllshire PA33 1AE
Tel: 01838 200370
Green Fee: ① 9 Holes 4528 yds SSS: 63
Visitors: Anyday Designer: McFarlane Barron Co.
Flat picturesque parkland course by River Orchay. Mountain views

Dunaverty (1889)

Southend, By Campbeltown, Argyllshire PA28 6RW
Tel: 01586 830677 Fax: 01586 830677
Green Fee: ① 18 Holes 4799 yds SSS: 63
Visitors: Anyday Designer: Unknown
Undulating hillside course with some great views

Gigha (1992)

Isle of Gigha, Kintyre, Argyllshire PA41 7AA
Tel: 01583 505254   Fax: 01583 505244

Green Fee: ①   9 Holes   5042 yds   SSS: 65
Visitors: Anyday   Designers: The Members
Links course with views of the Sound of Gigha and Kilberry Hills

Glencruitton (1901)

Glencruitton, Oban, Argyllshire PA34 4PU
Tel: 01631 562868   Pro: 01631 564115   Sec: 01631 564604

Green Fee: ②   18 Holes   4452 yds   SSS: 63
Visitors: Anyday   Designer: James Braid
Very hilly and testing downland course but well worth the effort

Inveraray (1893)

Inveraray, Argyllshire PA32 8UT
Tel: 01499 302140

Green Fee: ①   9 Holes   5760 yds   SSS: 68
Visitors: Anyday   Designers: Watt Landscaping
Although founded in 1893, this parkland course closed and re-opened in 1993

Isle of Eriska (1995)

Ledaig, by Oban, Argyllshire PA37 1SD
Tel: 01631 720802   Fax: 01631 720531

Green Fee: ①   9 Holes   3200 yds   SSS: 60
Visitors: Anyday   Designer: Unknown
Remote and very beautiful course set around hotel

Isle of Seil (1995)

Balvicar, by Oban, Argyllshire PA34 4TR
Tel: 01852 300348 or 300209

Green Fee: ①   9 Holes   4670 yds   SSS: 64
Visitors: Anyday   Designer: Founder Members
Flat coastal course with marvellous views of Seil Sound and hills of Ardmaddy

Area 6

Kyles of Bute (1907)

The Moss, Kames, Tighnabruaich, Argyllshire PA21 2BE
Tel: 01700 811603
Green Fee: ①   9 Holes   4778 yds   SSS: 64
Visitors: Anyday   Designer: Unknown
Moorland/heathland course with beautiful views. No bunkers but has streams running through

Lochgilphead (1891)

Blarbuie Road, Lochgilphead, Argyllshire PA31 8LE
Tel: 01546 602340

Green Fee: ①   9 Holes   4458 yds   SSS: 63
Visitors: Anyday   Designer: Dr. Ian MacCammond
Hilly parkland course

Lochgoilhead (1981)

Lochgoilhead, Argyllshire PA24 8AD
Tel: 01301 703435   Fax: 01301 703435
Green Fee: ①   9 Holes   3634 yds   SSS: 60
Visitors: Anyday   Designer: Unknown
Lochside parkland course alongside Loch Goil. Extremely scenic

Machrie (1891)

Machrie Hotel, Port Ellen, Isle of Islay PA42 7AN
Tel: 01496 302310   Fax: 01496 302404   Sec: 01496 302409

Green Fee: ③   18 Holes   6226 yds   SSS: 70
Visitors: Weekday   Designers: Willie Campbell/Donald Steel
Fabulous links course alongside Atlantic with lots of history

Machrihanish (1876)

Machrihanish, Campbeltown, Argyllshire PA28 6PT
Tel: 01586 810213   Fax: 01586 810221   Pro: 01586 810277

Green Fee: ③   18 Holes   6225 yds   SSS: 71
Visitors: Anyday
Designers: Tom Morris 1876, J. H. Taylor 1914, Sir Guy Campbell 1944
Fabulous challenging links course alongside Atlantic with lots of history. Natural beauty

Tarbert (1910)

Kilberry Road, Tarbert, Argyllshire PA29 6XX
Tel: 01546 606896
Green Fee: ①   9 Holes   4460 yds   SSS: 63
Visitors: Anyday   Designer: Unknown
Beautiful woodland course with streams running through

Taynuilt (1991)

Taynuilt, Argyllshire PA35 1JH
Tel: 01866 822429   Fax: 01866 822255
Green Fee: ①   9 Holes   4510 yds   SSS: 63
Visitors: Anyday   Designer: Unknown
Parkland course with stunning views across Loch Etive

Tobermory (1896)

Erray Road, Tobermory, Isle of Mull PA75 6PR
Tel: 01688 302338   Fax: 01688 302140
Green Fee: ①   9 Holes   4890 yds   SSS: 64
Visitors: Anyday   Designer: David Adams in 1935
Demanding hilly seaside clifftop course with superb views over the Sound of Mull

Vaul (1920)

Scarnish, Isle of Tiree, Argyllshire PA77 6TP
Tel: 01879 220334 or 220729
Green Fee: ①   9 Holes   5674 yds   SSS: 68
Visitors: Anyday   Designer: Unknown
Public seaside links course with stunning view from 4th tee

Area 6

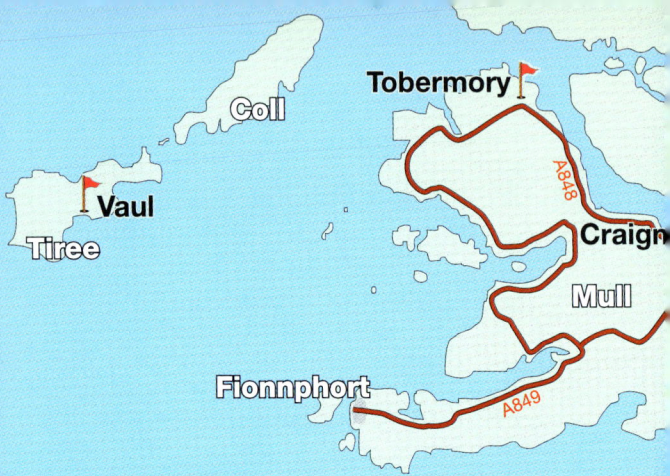

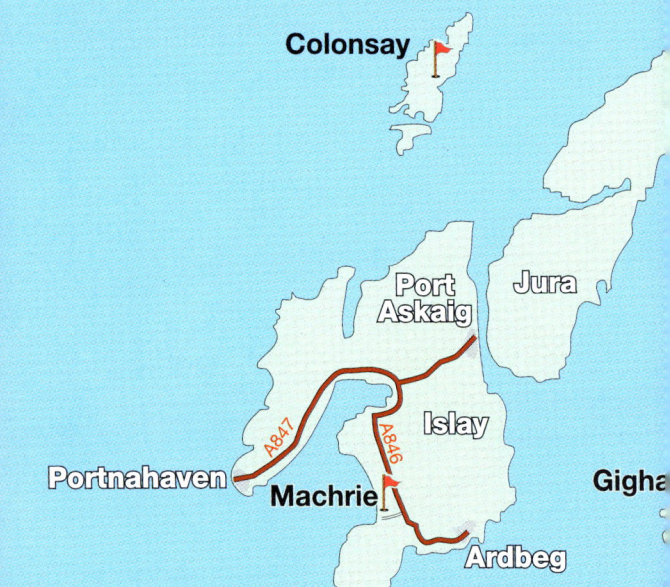

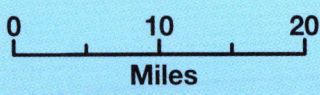

Tobermory

Coll

A848

Vaul

Craign

Tiree

Mull

Fionnphort

A849

Colonsay

Port Askaig

Jura

Islay

A847

A846

Portnahaven

Machrie

Gigha

Ardbeg

Machrihanis

Cam

0   10   20

Miles

Dunaver

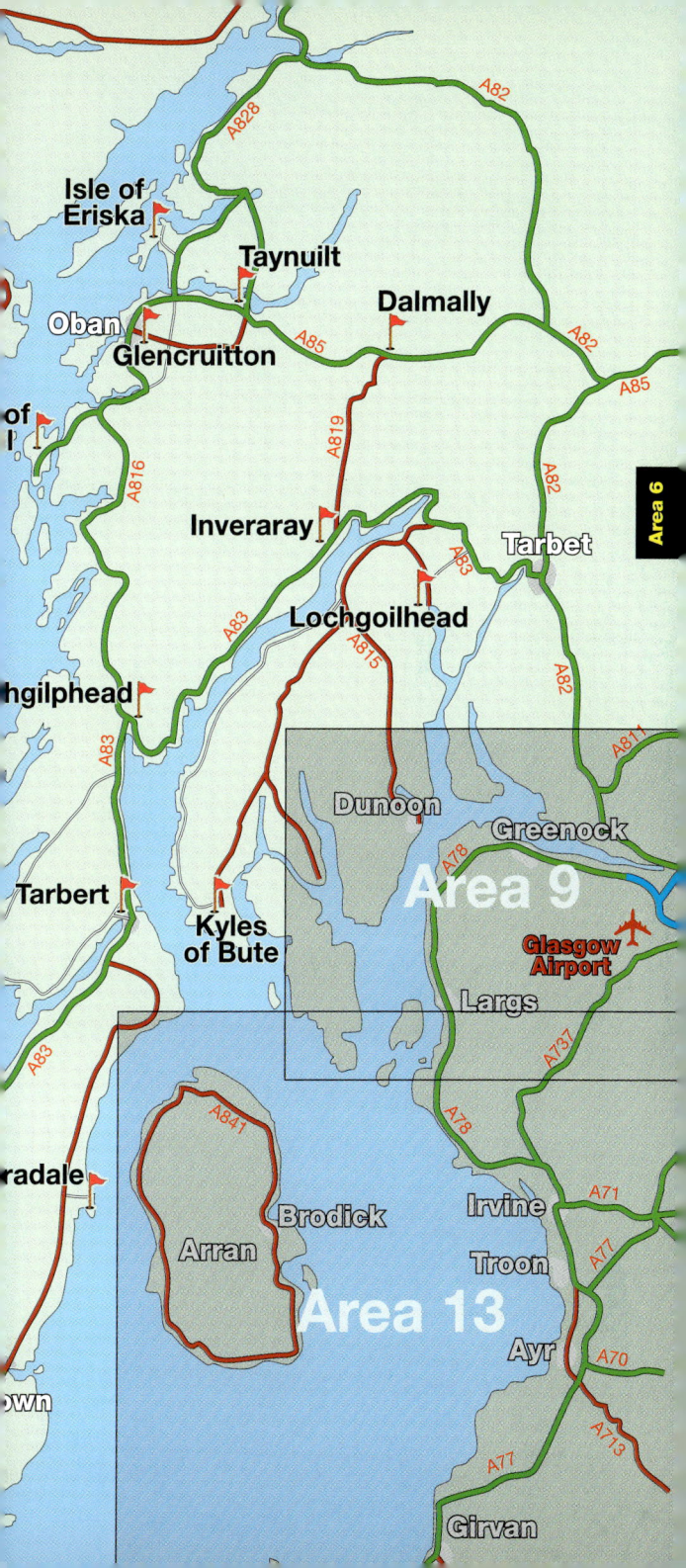

Isle of
Eriska

Taynuilt

Dalmally

Oban
Glencruitton

of
l

A828

A82

A85

A82

A85

A816

A819

A82

Inveraray

Tarbet

A83

Lochgoilhead

hgilphead

A83

A815

A82

A811

Dunoon

Greenock

A78

Area 9

Glasgow
Airport

Tarbert

Largs

Kyles
of Bute

A737

A83

A78

radale

A841

Irvine

A71

Brodick

Troon

A77

Arran

Area 13

Ayr

A70

own

A713

A77

Girvan

Aberfeldy (1895)

Taybridge Road, Aberfeldy, Perthshire PH15 2BH
Tel: 01887 820535   Fax: 01887 820535   Sec: 01887 820422
Green Fee: ①   18 Holes   5283 yds   SSS: 67
Visitors: Anyday   Designer: J. Souters

Parkland course situated by River Tay. Near famous Wade Bridge and Black Watch monument

Aberfoyle (1890)

Braeval, Aberfoyle, Stirlingshire FK8 3UY
Tel: 01786 382493
Green Fee: ①   18 Holes   5218 yds   SSS: 66
Visitors: Anyday   Designer: James Braid

Scenic heathland course with mountain views

Alloa (1891)

Schawpark, Sauchie, Clackmannanshire FK10 3AX
Tel: 01259 722745   Fax: 01259 724476 Pro: 01259 724476

Green Fee: ②   18 Holes   6229 yds   SSS: 71
Visitors: Anyday   Designer: James Braid

Beautiful parkland course with many scenic views

Alva (1900)

Beauclere Street, Alva, Clackmannanshire FK12 5LD
Tel: 01259 760431
Green Fee: ①   9 Holes   4910 yds   SSS: 64
Visitors: Anyday   Designer: Unknown

Undulating parkland course at foot of Ochil Hills

Auchterarder (1892)

Orchil Road, Auchterarder, Perthshire PH3 1LS
Tel: 01764 662804   Fax: 01764 662804   Pro: 01764 663711
Green Fee: ②   18 Holes   5775 yds   SSS: 68
Visitors: Anyday   Designer: Ben Sayers

Parkland course with fine views and lots of heather

Balfron (1994)

Kepculloch Road, Balfron, Stirlingshire G63 0QP
Tel: 01360 440915

Green Fee: ①   18 Holes   5940 yds   SSS: 69
Visitors: Anyday   Designer: Unknown
Undulating upland course with views of Campsie Fells

Braehead (1891)

Cambus, by Alloa, Clackmannanshire FK10 2NT
Tel: 01259 725766   Fax: 01259 214070   Pro: 01259 722078

Area 7

Green Fee: ②   18 Holes   6086 yds   SSS: 69
Visitors: Anyday   Designer: Robert Tait
Varied and interesting parkland course with scenic views

Bridge of Allan (1895)

Sunlaw, Bridge of Allan, Stirlingshire FK9 4LY
Tel: 01786 832332

Green Fee: ①   9 Holes   5120 yds   SSS: 65
Visitors: Anyday   Designer: Tom Morris
Very hilly parkland course with good views of Stirling Castle

Brucefields (1996)

Prinhall Road, Bannockburn, Stirlingshire FK7 8EH
Tel: 01786 818184   Fax: 01786 817770   Pro: 01786 818184

Green Fee: ①   9 Holes   5026 yds   SSS: 65
Visitors: Anyday   Designer: Souters Sportsturf
Rolling parkland course with fine views

Callander (1890)

Aveland Road, Callander, Perthshire FK17 8EN
Tel: 01877 330090   Fax: 01877 330062   Pro: 01877 330975

Green Fee: ②   18 Holes   5151 yds   SSS: 66
Visitors: Anyday   Designers: Tom Morris/Willie Fernie
Partly wooded parkland course with panoramic views

Canmore (1897)

Venturefair, Ave. Dunfermline, Fifeshire KY12 0PE
Tel: 01383 724969 or 726098   Pro: 01383 728416
Green Fee: ①   18 Holes   5376 yds   SSS: 66
Visitors: Anyday   Designers: Ben Sayers and others
Undulating parkland course

Comrie (1891)

Comrie, Perthshire PH6 2LR
Tel: 01764 670055 or 670941
Green Fee: ①   9 Holes   6040 yds   SSS: 70
Visitors: Anyday   Designer: Col. Williamson
Very scenic Highland course with excellent views

Craigie Hill (1909)

Cherrybank, Perth, Perthshire PH2 0NE
Tel: 01738 620829   Fax: 01738 620829   Pro: 01738 622644
Green Fee: ②   18 Holes   5386 yds   SSS: 67
Visitors: Anyday   Designers: W. Fernie/J. Anderson
Hilly parkland course with good views over Perth

Creiff (1891)

Perth Road, Creiff, Perthshire PH7 3LR
Tel: 01764 652397   Fax: 01764 655096   Pro: 01764 652909
Green Fee: ②   Ferntower   18 Holes   6402 yds   SSS: 72
         ①   Dornock   9 Holes   4772 yds   SSS: 63
Visitors: Anyday   Designer: James Braid
Both hilly parkland courses with magnificent views

Creiff Hydro (1893)

Ferntower Road, Creiff, Perthshire PH7 3LQ
Tel: 01764 651615 Fax: 01764 653087
Green Fee: ①   9 Holes   4536 yds   SSS: 64
Visitors: Anyday Designer: A. Brown, altered 1992: J. Freeman
Short hilly parkland course with wonderful views

Dollar (1890)

Brewlands House, Dollar, Clackmannanshire FK14 7EA
Tel: 01259 742400 Fax: 01259 743497 Pro: 01259 743581

Green Fee: ①   18 Holes   5242 yds   SSS: 66
Visitors: Anyday   Designer: Ben Sayers
Hillside course

Dunblane New (1923)

Perth Road, Dunblane, Perthshire FK15 0LJ
Tel: 01786 823711 Fax: 01786 821522 Pro: 01786 821521
Green Fee: ②   18 Holes   5930 yds   SSS: 69
Visitors: Weekdays   Designer: Unknown
Parkland course with some hard walking

Dunfermline (1887)

Pitfirrane, Crossford, Dunfermline, Fifeshire KY12 8QV
Tel: 01383 723534 Fax: 01383 723534 Pro: 01383 729061
Green Fee: ②   18 Holes   6121 yds   SSS: 70
Visitors: Weekdays   Designers: J. R. Stutt & Sons
Interesting parkland course with 16th century clubhouse

Dunkeld & Birnam (1892)

Fungarth, Dunkeld, Perthshire PH8 0HU
Tel: 01350 727524 Fax: 01350 728660
Green Fee: ②   18 Holes   5508 yds   SSS: 67
Visitors: Anyday   Designer: D. A. Tod
Interesting heathland course with wonderful views of the countryside

Dunning (1953)

Rollo Park, Dunning, Perthshire PH2 0RH
Tel: 01764 684747 Sec: 01764 684237
Green Fee: ①   9 Holes   4885 yds   SSS: 63
Visitors: Anyday   Designer: Unknown
Parkland course with burn meandering through

Forrester Park (2001)

Pitdinnie Road, Cairneyhill, Fifeshire KY12 8RF
Tel: 01383 880505   Fax: 01383 882505
Green Fee: ③   18 Holes   6296 yds   SSS: 72
Visitors: Anyday   Designer: Greens of Scotland
Undulating meadow course with views of Firth of Forth and Edinburgh

Gleneagles Hotel (1919)

Auchterarder, Perthshire PH3 1NF
Tel: 01764 662231   Fax: 01764 662134

Green Fee: ⑥   Kings   18 Holes   6790 yds   SSS: 73
           ⑥   Queens   18 Holes   5965 yds   SSS: 70
           ⑥   PGA Centenary 18 Holes   6559 yds   SSS: 73
Visitors: Anyday
Designers: James Braid (King and Queens)
           Jack Nicklaus (PGA)
Magnificent moorland undulating courses with heather,
bracken and pheasant. Equally magnificent hotel. Without a
doubt this is a must.
The PGA course opened in 1991

Green Hotel (1885, reopened 1991)

2 The Muirs, Kinross, Kinross-shire KY13 8AS
Tel: 01577 863407   Fax: 01577 863180   Pro: 01577 865125
Green Fee: ①   Red   18 Holes   6256 yds   SSS: 71
           ①   Blue   18 Holes   6438 yds   SSS: 72
Visitors: Anyday   Designer: Sir David Montgomery
Two interesting picturesque parkland courses with views over Loch Leven

Kenmore (1992)

Kenmore, Aberfeldy, Perthshire PH15 2HN
Tel: 01887 830226   Fax: 01887 830211
Green Fee: ①   9 Holes   6052 yds   SSS: 69
Visitors: Anyday   Designer: D. Menzies & Partners
Pay and play undulating parkland course alongside Loch Tay

Killin (1913)
Killin, Perthshire FK21 8TX
Tel: 01567 820312 Fax: 01567 820312
Green Fee: ①   9 Holes   5036 yds   SSS: 65
Visitors: Anyday   Designer: John Duncan
Parkland course in wonderful setting with very scenic views

King James VI (1858)
Moncreife Island, Perth, Perthshire PH2 8NR
Tel: 01738 632460 Fax: 01738 445132 Pro: 01738 632460
Green Fee: ②   18 Holes   6038 yds   SSS: 69
Visitors: Anyday   Designer: Tom Morris
Island parkland course in centre of Perth, surrounded by River Tay

Milnathort (1910)
South Street, Milnathort, Kinross-shire KY13 9XA
Tel: 01577 864069
Green Fee: ①   9 Holes   5985 yds   SSS: 69
Visitors: Anyday   Designer: Unknown
Undulating inland course

Area 7

Muckhart (1908)
Drumburn Road, Muckhart, Dollar, Clackmannanshire FK14 7JH
Tel: 01259 781423 Fax: 01259 781544 Pro: 01259 781493

Green Fee: ②   Muckhart   18 Holes   6058 yds   SSS: 70
          ①   Naemoor   9 Holes   6468 yds   SSS: 70
Visitors: Anyday   Designer: Unknown
Undulating scenic heathland course

Murrayshall Hotel (1981)
Scone, Perthshire PH2 7PH
Tel: 01738 554804 Fax: 01738 552595 Pro: 01738 552784
Green Fee: ③   Murrayshall   18 Holes   6441 yds   SSS: 72
          ②   Lynedoch   18 Holes   5359 yds   SSS: 68
Visitors: Anyday   Designer: J. Hamilton Strutt
One parkland, one woodland course. Very interesting

Muthill (1935)
Peat Road, Muthill, Perthshire PH5 2AD
Tel: 01764 681523 Fax: 01764 681557
Green Fee: ①   9 Holes   4742 yds   SSS: 63
Visitors: Anyday   Designer: Unknown
Parkland course with narrow fairways and pleasant views

North Inch (1897)
c/o Pullar House, 35 Kinnoull Street, Perth, Perthshire PH1 5GD
Tel: 01738 636481
Green Fee: ①   18 Holes   5718 yds   SSS: 65
Visitors: Anyday   Designer: Tom Morris
Pay and play tree-lined parkland course alongside the River Tay

Pitreavie (1922)
Queensferry Road, Dunfermline, Fifeshire KY11 5PR
Tel: 01383 722591   Fax: 01383 722591   Pro: 01383 723151
Green Fee: ②   18 Holes   6031 yds   SSS: 69
Visitors: Anyday   Designer: Dr. A. Mackenzie
Parkland and woodland course offering panoramic views of River Forth Valley

St. Fillans (1903)
South Loch Earn Road, St. Fillans, Perthshire PH6 2NJ
Tel: 01764 685312
Green Fee: ①   9 Holes   6054 yds   SSS: 69
Visitors: Anyday   Designer: James Braid
Beautiful parkland course with much flora and bird life

Saline (1912)
Kinneddar Hill, Saline, Fifeshire KY12 9LT
Tel: 01383 852591 or 852344
Green Fee: ①   9 Holes   5302 yds   SSS: 66
Visitors: Not Saturdays   Designer: Unknown
Hillside course with marvellous views of Forth Valley

Stirling (1869)
Queens Road, Stirling, Stirlingshire FK8 3AA
Tel: 01786 464098   Fax: 01786 450748   Pro: 01786 471490

Green Fee: ②   18 Holes   6438 yds   SSS: 71
Visitors: Anyday   Designer: James Braid
Extended by H. Cotton in 1967. Undulating parkland course

Strathtay (1909)
Lyon Cottage, Strathtay, Pitlochry, Perthshire PH9 0PG
Tel: 01887 840211
Green Fee: ①   9 Holes   4086 yds   SSS: 63
Visitors: Anyday   Designer: Unknown
Wooded hilly course with panoramic views

Taymouth Castle (1923)

Kenmore, By Aberfeldy, Tayside PH15 2NT
Tel: 01887 830228   Fax: 01887 830228

Green Fee: ②   18 Holes   6066 yds   SSS: 69
Visitors: Anyday   Designer: James Braid
Beautiful views in tranquil setting from this parkland course

Tillicoultry (1899)

Alva Road, Tillicoultry, Clackmannanshire FK13 6BL
Tel: 01259 750124 or 752934   Fax: 01259 752934

Green Fee: ①   9 Holes   5463 yds   SSS: 66
Visitors: Anyday   Designer: Peter Robinson
Parkland course at foot of Ochil Hills

Tulliallan (1902)

Alloa Road, Kincardine-on-Forth, Clackmannanshire FK10 4BB
Tel: 01259 730796   Fax: 01259 733950   Pro: 01259 730798
Green Fee: ①   18 Holes   5965 yds   SSS: 69
Visitors: Anyday   Designer: James Braid
Hilly parkland course

Whitemoss (1994)

Whitemoss Road, Dunning, Perthshire PH2 0QX
Tel: 01738 730300   Fax: 01738 730300
Green Fee: ①   18 Holes   5968 yds   SSS: 69
Visitors: Anyday   Designer: Whitemoss Leisure
Undulating meadowland course

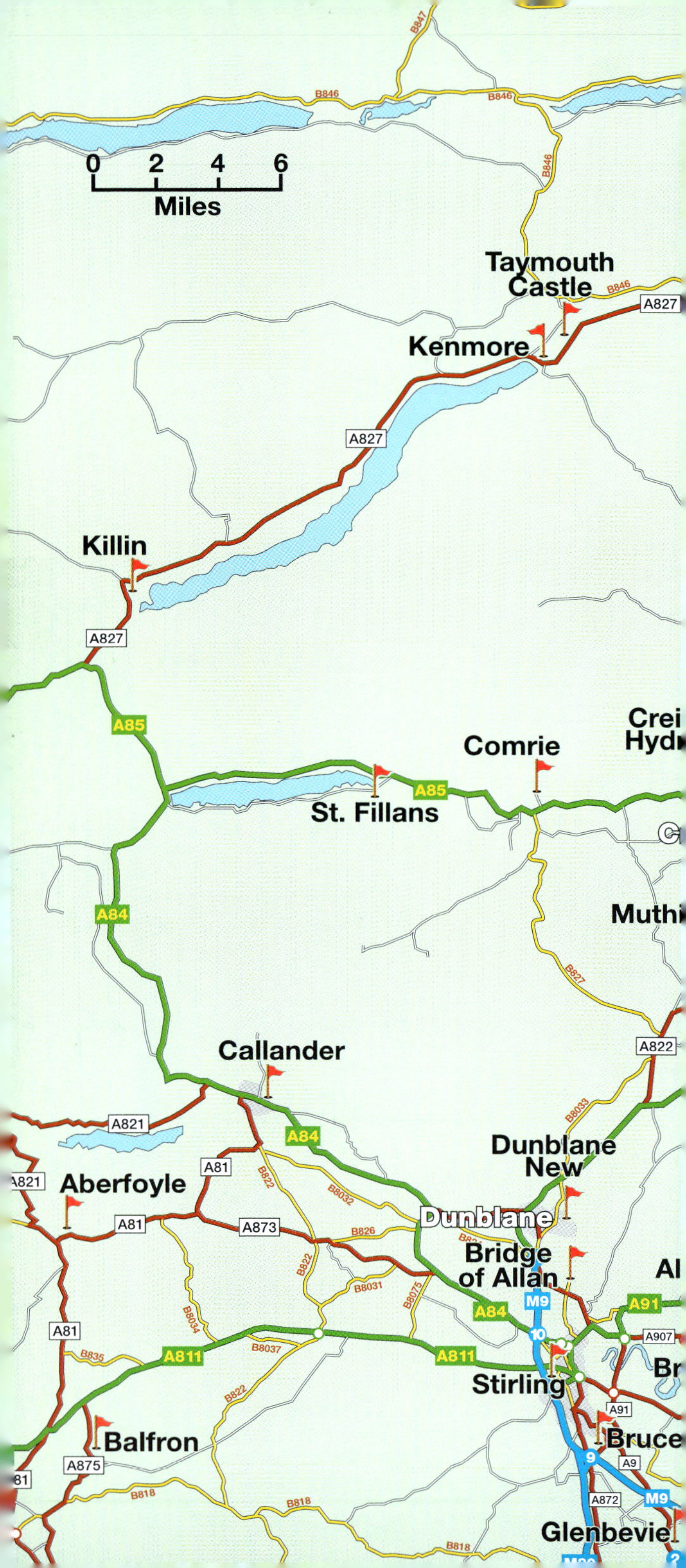

Scale

0 2 4 6
Miles

B846

B847

B846

B846

Taymouth
Castle

A827

Kenmore

A827

Killin

A827

A85

Comrie

Crei
Hyd

St. Fillans

A85

C

A84

Muthi

B827

Callander

A822

A821

A84

Dunblane
New

Aberfoyle

A81

B822

B8032

Dunblane

A821

A81

A81

A873

B826

Bridge
of Allan

Al

B802

B8031

B8075

A84

M9

A91

B8004

B835

A811

B8037

A811

10

Stirling

A907

Br

B822

A91

Bruce

Balfron

A875

81

B818

9

A9

A872

M9

B818

B818

Glenbevie

?

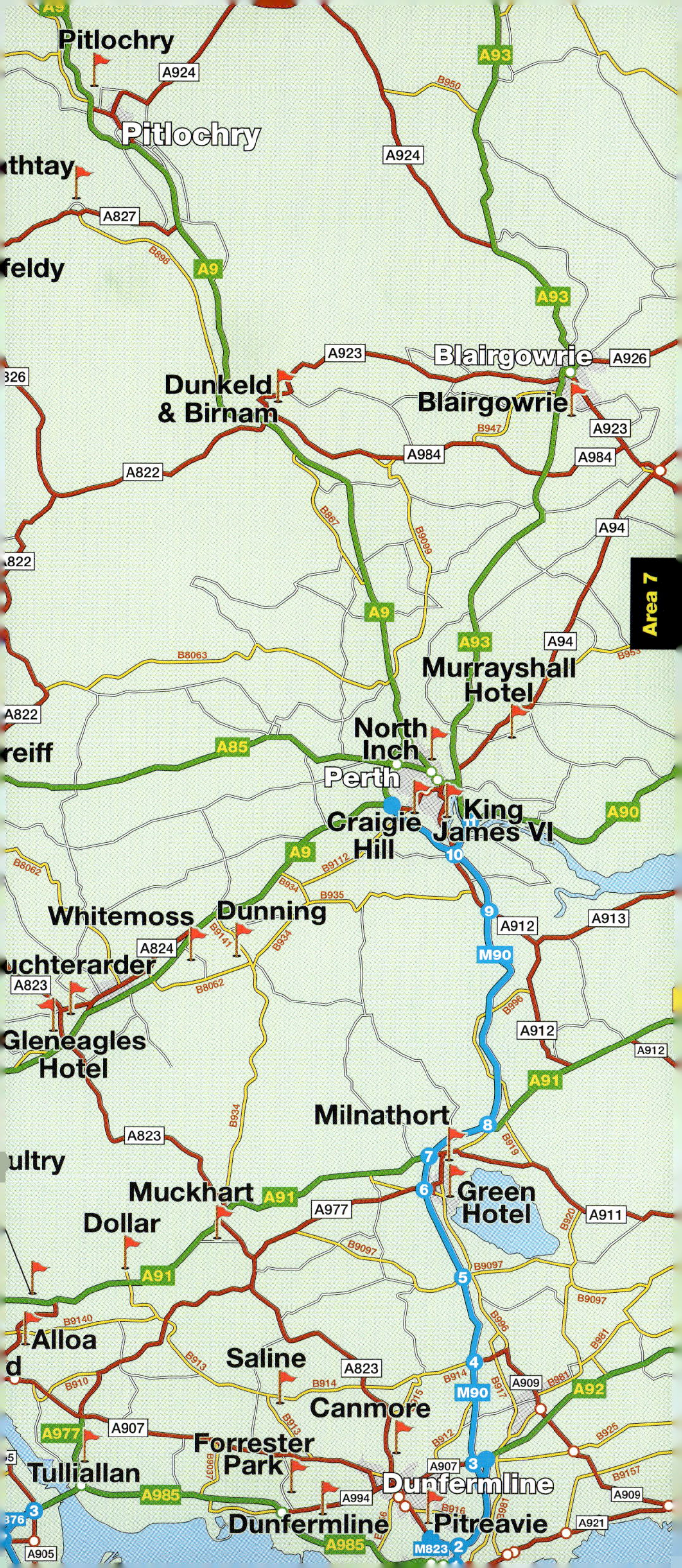

Pitlochry
A924
Pitlochry
ithtay
A827
B898
feldy
A9
A93
326
A923
Blairgowrie
A926
Dunkeld
& Birnam
Blairgowrie
A822
B947
A984
A984
A822
B867
B999
A94
822
A9
B8063
A93
A94
Murrayshall
Hotel
B953
A822
A85
North
Inch
A822
reiff
Perth
A90
Craigie
Hill
King
James VI
A9
B112
10
Whitemoss
B935
Dunning
B934
B8062
A824
B9141
B934
9
A912
A913
uchterarder
B8062
M90
A823
B596
Gleneagles
Hotel
A912
A912
A823
B934
Milnathort
A91
8
ultry
B819
7
Muckhart
A91
6
Green
Hotel
A911
Dollar
A977
B920
B9097
5
A91
B9097
B9097
Alloa
B9140
B888
B881
d
B910
B913
Saline
B914
A823
B914
M90
B817
A909
A92
Canmore
B881
A977
A907
B916
B912
Forrester
Park
A909
A907
B9157
Tulliallan
A994
Dunfermline
A909
A985
Dunfermline
Pitreavie
A921
376
3
A905
A985
M823
2

Aberdour (1896)

Seaside Place, Aberdour, Fifeshire KY3 0TX
Tel: 01383 860080   Fax: 01383 860050
Green Fee: ①   18 Holes   5460 yds   SSS: 66
Visitors: Anyday   Designers: P. Robertson/J. Anderson
Pretty parkland/seaside course with lovely views of the River Forth

Anstruther (1890)

Marsfield Shore Road, Anstruther, Fifeshire KY10 3DZ
Tel: 01333 310956 or 312283   Fax: 01333 312283
Green Fee: ①   9 Holes   4604 yds   SSS: 63
Visitors: Anyday   Designer: Tom Morris
Seaside links course

Auchterderran (1904)

Woodend Road, Cardenden, Fifeshire KY5 0NH
Tel: 01592 721579
Green Fee: ①   9 Holes   5250 yds   SSS: 66
Visitors: Anyday   Designer: Unknown
Pay and play parkland course

Balbirnie Park (1983)

Markinch, Glenrothes, Fifeshire KY7 6NR
Tel: 01592 612095   Fax: 01592 612383   Pro: 01592 752006

Green Fee: ②   18 Holes   6210 yds   SSS: 70
Visitors: Anyday   Designer: Fraser Middleton
Scenic undulating parkland course

Bishopshire (1903)
Kinnesswood, by Kinross, Tayside KY13 7HX
Tel: 01592 780203
Green Fee: ①   10 Holes   4218 yds   SSS: 64
Visitors: Anyday   Designer: Willie Park
Upland course with views across Loch Leven

Burntisland (1898)
Dodhead, Burntisland, Fifeshire KY3 9LQ
Tel: 01592 874093   Fax: 01592 873247   Pro: 01592 873247
Green Fee: ①   18 Holes   5965 yds   SSS: 70
Visitors: Anyday   Designer: James Braid
Parkland course with fine sea views

Charleton (1994)
Charleton, Colinsburgh, Fifeshire KY9 1HG
Tel: 01333 340505   Fax: 01333 340583   Pro: 01333 330009
Green Fee: ②   18 Holes   6149 yds   SSS: 70
Visitors: Anyday   Designer: John Salvesen
Wonderful views, this parkland course has streams & ditches in play

Cowdenbeath (1988)
Seco Place, Cowdenbeath, Fifeshire KY4 8PD
Tel: 01383 511918 or 313723   Fax: 01383 511918
Green Fee: ①   18 Holes   6552 yds   SSS: 71
Visitors: Anyday   Designer: Unknown
Public parkland course on site of old Dora coal mine – tree-lined fairways

Area 8

Crail (1786)
Balcomie Club House, Fifeness, Crail, Fifeshire KY10 3XN
Tel: 01333 450686   Fax: 01333 450416   Pro: 01333 450960

Green Fee: ③   Balcomie   18 Holes   5922 yds   SSS: 69
         ③   Craighead   18 Holes   6728 yds   SSS: 73
Visitors: Anyday   Designer: Tom Morris
Seventh oldest in the world. Very scenic testing links course on edge of North Sea

Cupar (1855)

Hilltarvit, Cupar, Fifeshire KY15 5JT
Tel: 01334 653549   Fax: 01334 653549   Sec: 01334 654101
Green Fee: ①   9 Holes   5074 yds   SSS: 65
Visitors: Anyday   Designer: Alan Robertson
Hillside parkland course with fine views

Drumoig (1996)

Leuchars, St. Andrews, Fifeshire KY16 0BE
Tel: 01382 541800   Fax: 01382 542211

Green Fee: ③   18 Holes   6742 yds   SSS: 72
Visitors: Anyday   Designer: Unknown
Parkland course with links feeling in parts

The Dukes (1995)

Craigtoun Park, St. Andrews, Fifeshire KY16 8NS
Tel: 01334 474371   Fax: 01334 477668

Green Fee: ④   18 Holes   6749 yds   SSS: 73
Visitors: Anyday   Designer: Peter Thomson
Parkland course with links feeling. Magnificent views of the bay of St. Andrews

Dunnikier Park (1963)

Dunnikier Way, Kirkcaldy, Fifeshire KY1 3LP
Tel: 01592 261599   Fax: 01592 642541   Pro: 01592 642121
Green Fee: ①   18 Holes   6709 yds   SSS: 72
Visitors: Anyday   Designer: R. Stutt
Parkland course with rolling fairways and pleasant views

Elie (1875)

Golf House Club, Elie, Leven, Fifeshire KY9 1AS
Tel: 01333 330301   Fax: 01333 330895   Pro: 01333 330955

Green Fee: ③   18 Holes   6273 yds   SSS: 70
Visitors: Anyday   Designer: Unknown
Home of James Braid. Delightful seaside links with panoramic views

Elie Sports Club (1908)

Elie, Leven, Fifeshire KY9 1AS
Tel: 01333 330955

Green Fee: ①   9 Holes   4354 yds   SSS: 64
Visitors: Anyday   Designer: Unknown
Excellent seaside links course

Elmwood (1998)

Stratheden, Nr. Cupar, Fifeshire KY15 5RS
Tel: 01334 658780   Fax: 01334 658781

Green Fee: ②   18 Holes   5951 yds   SSS: 68
Visitors: Anyday   Designer: Elmwood College
Parkland course with magnificent views of the Lomond Hills

Falkland (1976)

The Myre, Falkland, Cupar, Fifeshire KY14 7AA
Tel: 01337 857404

Green Fee: ①   9 Holes   4768 yds   SSS: 66
Visitors: Anyday   Designer: Unknown
Picturesque public parkland course with views of Falkland Palace

Glenrothes (1958)

Golf Course Road, Glenrothes, Fifeshire KY6 2LA
Tel: 01592 758686 or 750063 Fax: 01592 754561

Green Fee: ①   18 Holes   6444 yds   SSS: 71
Visitors: Anyday   Designer: J. R. Stutt & Sons
Public undulating parkland course with burn running through

Kinghorn (1887)

MacDuff Crescent, Kinghorn, Fifeshire KY3 9RF
Tel: 01592 890345   Fax: 01592 855761   Pro: 01592 890978

Green Fee: ①   18 Holes   5629 yds   SSS: 66
Visitors: Anyday   Designer: Tom Morris
Public undulating links course 300ft above the sea. Pleasant views

Kingsbarns (2000)

Kingsbarns, St. Andrews, Fifeshire KY16 8QD
Tel: 01334 460860   Fax: 01334 460877

Green Fee: ⑥   18 Holes   6652 yds   SSS: 72
Visitors: Anyday   Designers: Karl Phillips/Mark Parsinen
Wonderful new links course with views of the North Sea from every hole

Kirkcaldy (1904)

Balwearie Road, Kirkcaldy, Fifeshire KY2 5LT
Tel: 01592 205240   Fax: 01592 205240   Pro: 01592 203258
Green Fee: ②   18 Holes   6150 yds   SSS: 70
Visitors: Anyday   Designer: Tom Morris
Parkland course with beautiful views

Ladybank (1879)

Annsmuir, Ladybank, Fifeshire KY15 7RA
Tel: 01337 830814   Fax: 01337 831505   Pro: 01337 830725
Green Fee: ③   18 Holes   6580 yds   SSS: 72
Visitors: Anyday   Designer: Tom Morris
Heathland course with tall pines, thick heather and gorse

Leslie (1898)

Balsillie, Leslie, Fifeshire KY6 3EZ
Tel: 01592 620040

Green Fee: ①   9 Holes   4940 yds   SSS: 65
Visitors: Anyday   Designer: Tom Morris
Undulating parkland course

Leven Links (1846)

The Promenade, Links Road, Leven, Fifeshire KY8 4HS
Tel: 01333 428859 Fax: 01333 428859
Green Fee: ③   18 Holes   6434 yds   SSS: 70
Visitors: Anyday   Designer: Tom Morris
Classic seaside links course for Open Qualifying. Top class with undulating fairways and burns to cross

Lochgelly (1896)

Cartmore Road, Lochgelly, Fifeshire KY5 9PB
Tel: 01592 782589 or 780174
Green Fee: ①   18 Holes   5491 yds   SSS: 67
Visitors: Anyday   Designer: Ian Marchbanks (new 9 holes)
Challenging parkland course

Lochore Meadows (1981)

Crosshill, by Lochgelly, Fifeshire KY5 8BA
Tel: 01592 414300 Fax: 01592 414345
Green Fee: ①   9 Holes   6484 yds   SSS: 71
Visitors: Anyday   Designer: Fife Regional Council
Pay and play parkland course set alongside Loch Ore with natural stream running through

Lundin Ladies (1891)

Woodielea Road, Lundin Links, Fifeshire KY8 6AR
Tel: 01333 320832 or 320051
Green Fee: ①   9 Holes   4730 yds   SSS: 67
Visitors: Anyday   Designer: James Braid
Short course with coastal views

Area 8

Lundin Links (1868)

Golf Road, Lundin Links, Fifeshire KY8 6BA
Tel: 01333 320202 Fax: 01333 329743 Pro: 01333 320051

Green Fee: ③   18 Holes   6394 yds   SSS: 71
Visitors: Anyday   Designer: James Braid
Part seaside and part inland with a number of burns to cross

St. Andrews (14th century)

St. Andrews Links Trust, St. Andrews, Fifeshire KY16 9SF
Tel: 01334 466666   Fax: 01334 479555

Green Fee: (5)   Old Course   18 Holes   6566 yds   SSS: 72
Visitors: Designers: Nature with changes by Tom
Not Sundays   Morris/A. Robertson/A. MacKenzie

Green Fee: (1)   Balgove (1974)   9 Holes   3040 yds   SSS: 60
Visitors: Anyday   Designer: Donald Steel

Green Fee: (3)   Eden (1914)   18 Holes   6162 yds   SSS: 70
Visitors: Anyday   Designer: H. S. Colt

Green Fee: (3)   Jubilee (1989)   18 Holes   6805 yds   SSS: 73
Visitors: Anyday   Designer: J. Angus/Donald Steel

Green Fee: (3)   New Course (1895) 18 Holes   6604 yds   SSS: 72
Visitors: Anyday   Designer: Tom Morris

Green Fee: (2)   Strathyrum (1993) 18 Holes   5094 yds   SSS: 64
Visitors: Anyday   Designer: Donald Steel

The 'Home of Golf' where you play the most famous course in the world.
All St. Andrews courses are public

St. Andrews Bay (2001)

Kingask, St. Andrews, Fifeshire KY16 8PN
Tel: 01334 837000 Fax: 01334 471115

Green Fee: (5)   18 Holes   7020 yds   SSS: 73
Visitors: Anyday   Designer: Sam Torrance
Seaside links with views of St. Andrews town

St. Michaels (1903)

Gallowhill, Leuchars, Fifeshire KY16 0DX
Tel: 01334 838666   Fax: 01334 838666

Green Fee: ②   18 Holes   5802 yds   SSS: 68
Visitors: Anyday   Designer: Unknown
Undulating parkland course with views of Fife and Tayside

Scoonie (1951)

North Links, Leven, Fifeshire KY8 4SP
Tel: 01333 307007   Fax: 01333 307008   Pro: 01333 427437
Green Fee: ①   18 Holes   4979 yds   SSS: 65
Visitors: Anyday   Designer: Unknown
Inland public links course suitable for all standards

Area 8

Scotscraig (1817)

Golf Road, Tayport, Fifeshire DD6 9DZ
Tel: 01382 552515   Fax: 01382 553130   Pro: 01382 552855
Green Fee: ③   18 Holes   6550 yds   SSS: 72
Visitors: Anyday   Designer: Unknown
Heathland course with lots of heather. Used for Open Qualifying

Thornton (1921)

Station Road, Thornton, Fifeshire KY14 4DW
Tel: 01592 771111   Fax: 01592 774955   Pro: 01592 771173

Green Fee: ①   18 Holes   6155 yds   SSS: 69
Visitors: Anyday   Designer: The Members
Parkland course bounded by a river on three sides

Map

Dundee
A94
B953
A85
A90

Newburgh
A913
A92
A913
B936
B937
Elmwood
Cupar
A91
A91
Cup
B937
A914
Ladybank
B936
A912
A92
Falkland
A916
A927
Balbirnie Park
Bishopshire
A911
Leven
Leslie
Glenrothes
Glenrothes
Methil
B999
Lochore Meadows
B921
B9130
Thornton
B9097
A915
Auchterderran
B9130
B981
Lochgelly
A92
A955
B981
Cowdenbeath
Dunnikier Park
A910
Kirkcaldy
B925
Kirkcaldy
B9157
A921
Burntisland
A909
B923
Kinghorn
A921
Burntisland
Aberdour

Monifieth

Scotscraig

B946

Tayport

B945

Drumoig

A914

St. Michaels

A919

914

A91

St. Andrews • St Andrews

B939

The Dukes

St. Andrews Bay

A915

B9131

A917

Kingsbarns

B940

Crail

B841

B940

Area 8

B940

B9131

B9131

Crail

A915

Charleton

B9171

Anstruther

A917

B942

B942

Anstruther

din Links

Pittenweem

onnie

Elie

Elie Sports

en Links

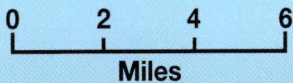

0   2   4   6
Miles

Area Nine

Beith (1896)

Threepwood Road, Beith, Ayrshire KA15 2JR
Tel: 01505 503166   Fax: 01505 506814
Green Fee: ①   18 Holes   5641 yds   SSS: 68
Visitors: Anyday   Designer: John Souter
Hilly course with panoramic views

Blairmore & Strone (1896)

High Road, Strone, by Dunoon, Argyllshire PA23 8JJ
Tel: 01369 840467 and 840676
Green Fee: ①   9 Holes   4400 yds   SSS: 62
Visitors: Anyday   Designer: James Braid
Undulating moorland/parkland course with great views of the Clyde

Buchanan Castle (1936)

Drymen, Stirlingshire G63 0HY
Tel: 01360 660307   Fax: 01360 660382   Pro: 01360 660330
Green Fee: ③   18 Holes   6086 yds   SSS: 69
Visitors: Anyday   Designer: James Braid
Parkland course with pleasant views

Bute (1888)

Kingarth, Rothesay, Isle of Bute, Argyllshire PA20 0BG
Tel: 01700 504369   Fax: 01700 504369
Green Fee: ①   9 Holes   4994 yds   SSS: 64
Visitors: Anyday   Designer: Unknown
Seaside links course with fenced greens. Pleasant views

Caldwell (1903)

Uplawnmoor, Renfrewshire G78 4AU
Tel: 01505 850329 Fax: 01505 850604 Pro: 01505 850616
Green Fee: ②   18 Holes   6228 yds   SSS: 70
Visitors: Weekdays   Designer: Willie Fernie
Moorland/parkland course

Cardross (1895)

Main Road, Cardross, Dumbartonshire G82 5LB
Tel: 01389 841754   Fax: 01389 842162   Pro: 01389 841350
Green Fee: ③   18 Holes   6469 yds   SSS: 72
Visitors: Anyday   Designers: James Braid 1921/W. Fernie 1904
Challenging undulating parkland course with views

Clydebank Municipal (1927)

Overtoun Road, Clydebank, Dumbartonshire G81 3RE
Tel: 0141 952 8698 Fax: 0141 952 6372 Pro: 0141 952 6372
Green Fee: ①   18 Holes   5349 yds   SSS: 66
Visitors: Anyday   Designer: Unknown
Public parkland course

Cochrane Castle (1895)

Scott Avenue, Craigston, Johnstone, Renfrewshire PA5 0HF
Tel: 01505 320146   Fax: 01505 325338   Pro: 01505 328465
Green Fee: ②   18 Holes   6226 yds   SSS: 71
Visitors: Weekdays   Designer: Charles Hunter/James Braid
Hilly, wooded course with streams running through

Cowal (1891)

Ardenslate Road, Dunoon, Argyllshire PA23 8NN
Tel: 01369 705673   Fax: 01369 705673   Pro: 01369 702395
Green Fee: ②   18 Holes   6063 yds   SSS: 70
Visitors: Anyday   Designer: James Braid 1928
Moorland course with panoramic views

Dumbarton (1888)

Broad Meadow, Dumbarton, Dumbartonshire G82 2BQ
Tel: 01389 732830   Fax: 01389 765995
Green Fee: ②   18 Holes   6017 yds   SSS: 69
Visitors: Weekdays   Designer: Unknown
Flat parkland course

Elderslie (1909)

63 Main Street, Elderslie, Renfrewshire PA5 9AZ
Tel: 01505 323956   Fax: 01505 340346   Pro: 01505 320032
Green Fee: ②   18 Holes   6175 yds   SSS: 70
Visitors: Weekdays   Designer: James Braid
Undulating parkland course with views

Erskine (1904)

Bishopton, Renfrewshire PA7 5PH
Tel: 01505 862302   Fax: 01505 862898   Pro: 01505 862108
Green Fee: ②   18 Holes   6287 yds   SSS: 70
Visitors: Weekdays   Designer: Unknown
Parkland course

Fereneze (1904)

Fereneze Avenue, Barrhead, Renfrewshire G78 1HJ
Tel: 0141 887 4141   Fax: 0141 881 7149   Pro: 0141 880 7058
Green Fee: ②   18 Holes   5962 yds   SSS: 70
Visitors: Weekdays   Designer: Unknown
Hilly moorland course

Gleddoch (1974)

Old Greenock Road, Langbank, Renfrewshire PA14 6YE
Tel: 01475 540304   Fax: 01475 540201   Pro: 01475 540704

Green Fee: ③   18 Holes   6283 yds   SSS: 71
Visitors: Anyday   Designer: J. Hamilton Stutt
Park/heathland course with fine views of Firth of Forth

Gourock (1896)

Cowal View, Gourock, Renfrewshire PA19 1HD
Tel: 01475 631001   Fax: 01475 638307   Pro: 01475 636834

Green Fee: ②   18 Holes   6512 yds   SSS: 73
Visitors: Anyday   Designer: Sir Henry Cotton
Hilly moorland course with magnificent views over Firth of Clyde

Greenock (1890)

Forsyth Street, Greenock, Renfrewshire PA16 8RE
Tel: 01475 720793   Fax: 01475 791912   Pro: 01475 787236
Green Fee: ②   18 Holes   5888 yds   SSS: 69
Visitors: Anyday   Designer: James Braid
Moorland course with views of the Clyde estuary, also has a 9 hole course

Greenock Whinhill (1911)

Beith Road, Greenock, Renfrewshire PA16 9LN
Tel: 01475 721064 or 724694
Green Fee: ①   18 Holes   5504 yds   SSS: 68
Visitors: Anyday   Designer: Willie Fernie
Public picturesque heathland course

Helensburgh (1893)

25 East Abercromby Street, Helensburgh, Dumbartonshire G84 9HZ
Tel: 01436 674173   Fax: 01436 671170   Pro: 01436 675505

Green Fee: ②   18 Holes   6104 yds   SSS: 70
Visitors: Weekdays   Designer: Tom Morris
Meadowland course with super views of Loch Lomond and River Clyde

Innellan (1881)

Knockamille Road, Innellan, Argyllshire PA23 7SG
Tel: 01369 830242
Green Fee: ①   9 Holes   4686 yds   SSS: 64
Visitors: Anyday   Designer: Unknown
Hilltop parkland course with views over Firth of Clyde

Kilbirnie Place (1922)

Largs Road, Kilbirnie, Ayrshire KA25 7AT
Tel: 01505 68444 or 683398
Green Fee: ①   18 Holes   5411 yds   SSS: 67
Visitors: Not Saturdays   Designer: Unknown
Easy walking parkland course. Pleasant views of countryside and Place Castle

Kilmacolm (1890)

Porterfield Road, Kilmacolm, Renfrewshire PA13 4PD
Tel: 01505 872139   Fax: 01505 874007   Pro: 01505 872695
Green Fee: ②   18 Holes   5961 yds   SSS: 69
Visitors: Anyday   Designer: James Braid
Moorland course with views

Largs (1891)

Irvine Road, Largs, Ayrshire KA30 8EU
Tel: 01475 673594   Fax: 01475 673594   Pro: 01475 686192
Green Fee: ③   18 Holes   6237 yds   SSS: 71
Visitors: Anyday   Designer: Unknown
A parkland tree-lined course. Pleasant views of the coast and Arran

Area 9

Loch Lomond (1993)

Rossdhu House, Luss, Dumbartonshire G83 8NT
Tel: 01436 655555   Fax: 01436 655500

Green Fee: ⑦   18 Holes   7060 yds   SSS: 72
Visitors: Members Guests only   Designers: Tom Weiskof & Jay Morrish
Wonderful parkland course on the 'Bonnie bonnie banks of Loch Lomond' with marvellous views of Ben Lomond

Lochwinnoch (1897)

Burnfoot Road, Lochwinnoch, Renfrewshire PA12 4AN
Tel: 01505 842153   Fax: 01505 843668   Pro: 01505 843029
Green Fee: ②   18 Holes   6243 yds   SSS: 71
Visitors: Anyday   Designer: Unknown
Scenic parkland course with natural burns running through

Millport (1888)

Millport, Isle of Cumbrae KA28 0HB
Tel: 01475 530306   Fax: 01475 530306   Pro: 01475 530305

Green Fee: ②   18 Holes   5828 yds   SSS: 69
Visitors: Anyday   Designer: James Braid
A pleasant seaside moorland course situated on west side of Isle of Cumbrae

Old Course Ranfurly (1905)

Ranfurly Place, Bridge of Weir, Renfrewshire PA11 3DE
Tel: 01505 613612 or 613614   Fax: 01505 613214
Green Fee: ②   18 Holes   6089 yds   SSS: 70
Visitors: Weekdays   Designer: Willie Park
Demanding inland hillside course

Paisley (1895)

Braehead, Paisley, Renfrewshire PA2 8TZ
Tel: 0141 884 3903   Fax: 0141 884 3903   Pro: 0141 884 4114
Green Fee: ②   18 Holes   6466 yds   SSS: 72
Visitors: Weekdays   Designer: J. Stutt
Moorland course with fine views

Port Bannatyne (1912)

Bannatyne Mains Road, Port Bannatyne, Isle of Bute PA20 0PH
Tel: 01700 504544
Green Fee: ①   13 Holes   5085 yds   SSS: 65
Visitors: Anyday   Designer: Peter Morrison
Hilly seaside course with panoramic views

Port Glasgow (1895)

Devol Farm, Port Glasgow, Renfrewshire PA14 5XE
Tel: 01475 704181 or 791214
Green Fee: ①   18 Holes   5712 yds   SSS: 68
Visitors: Anyday   Designer: Unknown
Moorland course situated on hilltop overlooking the Clyde

Ranfurly Castle (1889)

Golf Road, Bridge of Weir, Renfrewshire PA11 3HN
Tel: 01505 612609   Fax: 01505 610406   Pro: 01505 614795
Green Fee: ③   18 Holes   6284 yds   SSS: 71
Visitors: Weekdays Designers: Andrew Kirkaldy/Willie Auchterlonie
Picturesque moorland/heathland course

Rothesay (1892)

Canada Hill, Rothesay, Isle of Bute PA20 9HN
Tel: 01700 502244   Fax: 01700 503554   Pro: 01700 503554

Green Fee: ①   18 Holes   5419 yds   SSS: 66
Visitors: Anyday   Designers: James Braid/Ben Sayers
Hilly parkland course. Very scenic with views from every hole

Area 9

Routenburn (1914)

Greenock Road, Largs, Ayrshire KA30 9AH
Tel: 01475 673230   Fax: 01475 687240   Pro: 01475 687240
Green Fee: ①   18 Holes   5604 yds   SSS: 68
Visitors: Anyday   Designer: James Braid
Heathland course with views of the Firth of Clyde

Skelmorlie (1891)

Skelmorlie, Ayrshire PA17 5ES
Tel: 01475 520152
Green Fee: ①   18 Holes   5030 yds   SSS: 65
Visitors: Anyday   Designer: James Braid
Parkland/moorland course with magnificent views over the Firth of Clyde

Strathendrick (1901)

Glasgow Road, Drymen, Stirlingshire G63 0BY
Tel: 01360 660695 or 660675
Green Fee: ①   9 Holes   5116 yds   SSS: 64
Visitors: Weekdays   Designer: Unknown
Hilly moorland course

Vale of Leven (1907)

Northfield Road, Bonhill, Alexandria, Dumbartonshire G83 9ET
Tel: 01389 752351   Sec: 01389 757691   Pro: 01389 775012
Green Fee: ①   18 Holes   5167 yds   SSS: 66
Visitors: Anyday   Designer: Unknown
Hilly moorland course with gorse and burns. Overlooking Loch Lomond

A886

A815

A814

B833

B833

Blairmore
& Strone

B836

A815

A880

A815

Cowal

A885

Dunoon

Gourock

Gr

A770

A78

Gre
W

Innellan

A815

A886

Port
Bannatyne

B875

Skelmorlie

A844

Rothesay

A78

Rothesay

B878

Routenburn

A844

B881

Largs

A78

Largs

A844

B896

A760

Bute

B896

B881

Millport

B896

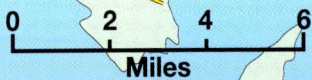

0   2   4   6

Miles

A78

Loch Lomond

Buchanan Castle

Strathendrick

B837

A817

A82

A809

Helensburgh

B831

A811

B832

Helensburgh

Vale of Leven

A814

Alexandria

Bonhill

Cardross

B857

A813

Greenock

Dumbarton

Dumbarton

A814

A82

Port Glasgow

31

Erskine

A814

Port Glasgow

A8

Gleddoch

Clydebank Municipal

A8014

A761

A8

B788

30

M8

A726

A8

Kilmacolm

B789

Ranfurly Castle

B790

28A

28

27

Old Course Ranfurly

B789

29

Paisley

A761

Elderslie

B786

B774

Cochrane Castle

A737

Paisley

Lochwinoch

B776

B775

Fereneze

A760

A736

birnie 'lace

Beith

Caldwell

B784

B777

B777

B706

A737

B709

Alexandra Park (1880)

Alexandra Park, Dennistown, Glasgow G31 8SE
Tel: 0141 556 1294   Pro: 0141 770 0519

Green Fee: ①   9 Holes   4562 yds   SSS: 62
Visitors: Anyday   Designer: Graham McArthur

Hilly parkland course

Balmore (1906)

Golf Course Road, Balmore, Glasgow G64 4AW
Tel: 01360 620284 or 620240   Fax: 01360 620284

Green Fee: ②   18 Holes   5542 yds   SSS: 67
Visitors: Weekdays   Designer: James Braid

Parkland course with pleasant views

Barshaw (1920)

Glasgow Road, Paisley, Renfrewshire PA2 3TJ
Tel: 0141 889 2908   Fax: 0141 840 2148

Green Fee: ①   18 Holes   5703 yds   SSS: 67
Visitors: Anyday   Designer: Unknown

Public parkland course

Bearsden (1891)

Thorn Road, Bearsden, Glasgow G61 4BP
Tel: 0141 942 2351

Green Fee: ①   9 Holes   6014 yds   SSS: 69
Visitors: Anyday   Designer: Unknown

Parkland course with views over the city

Bishopbriggs (1906)

Brackenbrae Road, Bishopbriggs, Glasgow G64 2DX
Tel: 0141 772 8938   Fax: 0141 762 2532
Green Fee: ②   18 Holes   6041 yds   SSS: 69
Visitors: Weekdays   Designer: James Braid
Parkland course with views of the Campsie Hills

Blairbeth (1910)

Fernbrae Avenue, Burnside, Rutherglen, Glasgow G73 4SF
Tel: 0141 634 3325 or 3355
Green Fee: ②   18 Holes   5518 yds   SSS: 68
Visitors: Weekdays   Designer: Unknown
Parkland course

Bothwell Castle (1922)

Blantyre Road, Bothwell, Glasgow G71 8PS
Tel: 01698 853177   Fax: 01698 854052   Pro: 01698 852052
Green Fee: ②   18 Holes   6243 yds   SSS: 70
Visitors: Weekdays   Designer: Unknown
Tree-lined mature parkland course

Calderbraes (1891)

57 Roundknowe Road, Uddingston, Glasgow G71 7TS
Tel: 01698 813425   Sec: 0141 773 2287
Green Fee: ②   9 Holes   5046 yds   SSS: 67
Visitors: Weekdays   Designer: Unknown
Hilly parkland course with good views

Cambuslang (1892)

30 Westburn Drive, Cambuslang, Glasgow G72 7NA
Tel: 0141 641 3130
Green Fee: ①   9 Holes   6072 yds   SSS: 69
Visitors: Weekdays   Designer: Unknown
Parkland course

Campsie (1897)

Crow Road, Lennoxtown, Glasgow G66 7HX
Tel: 01360 310244   Pro: 01360 310920
Green Fee: ①   18 Holes   5517 yds   SSS: 68
Visitors: Weekdays   Designer: Willie Auchterlonie
Scenic hillside parkland course

Cathcart Castle (1895)

Mearns Road, Clarkston, Glasgow G76 7YL
Tel: 0141 638 0082   Fax: 0141 638 1201   Pro: 0141 638 3436
Green Fee: ③   18 Holes   5832 yds   SSS: 68
Visitors: Anyday   Designer: Unknown
Undulating tree-lined parkland course

Cathkin Braes (1888)

Cathkin Road, Rutherglen, Glasgow G73 4SE
Tel: 0141 634 6605   Fax: 0141 630 9186   Pro: 0141 634 0650
Green Fee: ②   18 Holes   6208 yds   SSS: 71
Visitors: Weekdays   Designer: James Braid
Moorland course

Cawder (1933)

Cadder Road, Bishopbriggs, Glasgow G64 3QD
Tel: 0141 772 7101   Fax: 0141 772 4463

Green Fee: ③   Cawder   18 Holes   6297 yds   SSS: 71
        ③   Keir   18 Holes   5871 yds   SSS: 68
Visitors: Weekdays Designers: James Braid (Cawder)/Steel (Keir)
Two parkland courses. Cawder is hilly while Keir is flat

Clober (1951)

Craigton Road, Milngavie, Glasgow G62 7HP
Tel: 0141 956 1685 Fax: 0141 955 1416 Pro: 0141 956 6963
Green Fee: ①   18 Holes   4963 yds   SSS: 65
Visitors: Weekdays   Designer: Lyle Family
Parkland course

Clydebank & District (1905)

Hardgate, Clydebank, Dumbartonshire G81 5QY
Tel: 01389 383833   Fax: 01389 383831   Pro: 01389 383835
Green Fee: ①   18 Holes   5825 yds   SSS: 68
Visitors: Weekdays   Designer: Committee Members
Undulating parkland course

Coatbridge (1971)

Townhead Road, Coatbridge, Lanarkshire ML5 2HX
Tel: 01236 428975 or 426811   Pro: 01236 421492
Green Fee: ①   18 Holes   6026 yds   SSS: 69
Visitors: Anyday   Designer: Unknown
Public parkland course

Cowglen (1906)

301 Barrhead Road, Glasgow G43 1EU
Tel: 0141 632 0556 Fax: 0141 636 5411 Pro: 0141 649 9401
Green Fee: ②   18 Holes   6079 yds   SSS: 70
Visitors: Weekdays   Designer: David Adams/James Braid
Undulating parkland course with views of the Clyde valley

Crow Wood (1925)

Cumbernauld Road, Muirhead, Glasgow G69 9JF
Tel: 0141 779 4954 Fax: 0141 779 9148 Pro: 0141 779 1943
Green Fee: ②   18 Holes   6261 yds   SSS: 71
Visitors: Weekdays   Designer: James Braid
Parkland course

Douglas Park (1897)

Hillfoot, Bearsden, Glasgow G61 2TJ
Tel: 0141 942 0985   Fax: 0141 942 0985   Pro: 0141 942 1482

Green Fee: ②   18 Holes   5962 yds   SSS: 69
Visitors: Weekdays   Designer: Willie Fernie
Undulating parkland course

Drumpellier (1894)

Drumpellier Avenue, Coatbridge, Lanarkshire ML5 1RX
Tel: 01236 424139   Fax: 01236 428723   Pro: 01236 432971
Green Fee: ③   18 Holes   6277 yds   SSS: 70
Visitors: Weekdays   Designer: Willie Fernie
Parkland course

East Kilbride (1900)

Chapelside Road, Nerston, Lanarkshire G74 4PF
Tel: 01355 247728   Pro: 01355 22192
Green Fee: ②   18 Holes   6402 yds   SSS: 71
Visitors: Weekdays   Designer: Fred Hawtree
Challenging parkland course

East Renfrewshire (1922)

Loganswell, Pilmuir, Newton Mearns, Glasgow G77 6RT
Tel: 01355 500256   Fax: 01355 500323   Pro: 01355 500206

Green Fee: ③   18 Holes   6097 yds   SSS: 70
Visitors: Weekdays   Designer: James Braid
Moorland course beside Loch

Esporta Douglaston (1974)

Strathblane Road, Milngavie, Glasgow G62 8HJ
Tel: 0141 955 2434   Fax: 0141 955 2406   Pro: 0141 955 2404
Green Fee: ②   18 Holes   6040 yds   SSS: 69
Visitors: Anyday   Designer: John Harris
Challenging parkland course with streams and ditches

Glasgow (1787)

Killermont, Bearsden, Glasgow G61 2TW
Tel: 0141 942 2011   Fax: 0141 942 0770   Pro: 0141 942 8507

Green Fee: ③   18 Holes   5977 yds   SSS: 69
Visitors: Weekdays   Designer: Tom Morris
Parkland course with wide fairways, eighth oldest club in the world

Haggs Castle (1910)

70 Dumbreck Road, Dumbreck, Glasgow G41 4SN
Tel: 0141 427 1157   Fax: 0141 427 1157   Pro: 0141 427 3355
Green Fee: ③   18 Holes   6419 yds   SSS: 71
Visitors: Weekdays
Designers: James Braid, redesigned 1973 by Alliss/Thomas
Difficult wooded parkland course

Hayston (1926)

Campsie Road, Kirkintilloch, Glasgow G66 1RN
Tel: 0141 776 1244   Fax: 0141 776 9030   Pro: 0141 775 0882

Green Fee: ②   18 Holes   6052 yds   SSS: 70
Visitors: Weekdays   Designer: James Braid
Undulating tree-lined parkland course

Hilton Park (1927)

Stockiemuir Road, Milngavie, Glasgow G62 7HB
Tel: 0141 956 4657 Fax: 0141 956 4657 Pro: 0141 956 5125
Green Fee: ② Hilton   18 Holes   6054 yds   SSS: 70
           ② Allander 18 Holes   5487 yds   SSS: 67
Visitors: Weekdays Designer: James Braid
Moorland course with magnificent scenery

Kilsyth Lennox (1900)

Tak-Me-Doon Road, Kilsyth, Glasgow G65 0RS
Tel: 01236 823213 or 824115 Fax: 01236 823089
Green Fee: ①   18 Holes   5930 yds   SSS: 70
Visitors: Anyday   Designer: Unknown
Hilly moorland course

Kings Park (1934)

150a Croftpark Avenue, Croftfoot, Glasgow G54 0DD
Tel: 0141 630 1597 Fax: 0141 630 1597
Green Fee: ①   9 Holes   4236 yds   SSS: 60
Visitors: Anyday   Designer: Unknown
Heathland course

Kirkhill (1910)

Greenlees Road, Cambuslang, Glasgow G72 8YN
Tel: 0141 641 8499 Fax: 0141 641 8499 Pro: 0141 641 7972
Green Fee: ②   18 Holes   6030 yds   SSS: 70
Visitors: Weekdays   Designer: James Braid
Moorland course

Kirkintilloch (1894)

Campsie Road, Kirkintilloch, Glasgow G66 1RN
Tel: 0141 776 1256 Fax: 0141 775 2424 Sec: 0141 775 2387
Green Fee: ②   18 Holes   5860 yds   SSS: 69
Visitors: Weekdays   Designer: James Braid
Parkland course in rural setting

Area 10

Knightswood (1920)

Lincoln Avenue, Knightswood, Glasgow G13 3DN
Tel: 0141 959 6358

Green Fee: ①   9 Holes   5586 yds   SSS: 67
Visitors: Anyday   Designer: Unknown
Public parkland course

Lenzie (1889)

19 Crosshill Road, Lenzie, Glasgow G66 5DA
Tel: 0141 812 3018   Fax: 0141 812 3018   Pro: 0141 777 7748
Green Fee: ②   18 Holes   5984 yds   SSS: 69
Visitors: Weekdays   Designer: Unknown
Pleasant parkland course

Lethamhill (1933)

1240 Cumbernauld Road, Millerston, Glasgow G33 1AH
Tel: 0141 770 6220   Fax: 0141 770 0520
Green Fee: ①   18 Holes   5836 yds   SSS: 69
Visitors: Weekdays   Designer: Unknown
Public parkland course

Linn Park (1924)

Simshill Road, Cathcart, Glasgow G44 5TA
Tel: 0141 633 0377
Green Fee: ①   18 Holes   5005 yds   SSS: 66
Visitors: Anyday   Designer: Glasgow Parks
Public parkland course

Littlehill (1926)

Auchinairn Road, Bishopbriggs, Glasgow G64 1UT
Tel: 0141 772 1916
Green Fee: ①   18 Holes   6228 yds   SSS: 70
Visitors: Anyday   Designer: James Braid
Public parkland course

Milngavie (1895)

Laighpark, Milngavie, Glasgow G62 8EP
Tel: 0141 956 1619   Fax: 0141 956 4252
Green Fee: ②   18 Holes   5818 yds   SSS: 68
Visitors: Anyday   Designer: James Braid
Scenic and challenging moorland course

Mount Ellen (1905)

Lochend Road, Gartcosh, Glasgow G69 9EY
Tel: 01236 872277   Fax: 01236 872249   Pro: 01236 872632
Green Fee: ①   18 Holes   5525 yds   SSS: 68
Visitors: Anyday   Designer: Unknown
Testing parkland course with lots of bunkers

Pollock (1892)

90 Barrhead Road, Pollock, Glasgow G43 1BG
Tel: 0141 632 4351   Fax: 0141 649 1398
Green Fee: ③   18 Holes   6358 yds   SSS: 70
Visitors: Anyday   Designer: James Braid
Wooded parkland course alongside a river

Ralston (1904)

Strathmore Avenue, Ralston, Paisley, Renfrewshire PA1 3DT
Tel: 0141 882 1349   Fax: 0141 883 9837   Pro: 0141 810 4925
Green Fee: ②   18 Holes   6091 yds   SSS: 69
Visitors: Anyday   Designer: James Braid
Parkland course

Renfrew (1894)

Blythwood Estate, Inchinnan Road, Renfrewshire PA4 9EG
Tel: 0141 886 6692   Fax: 0141 886 1808   Pro: 0141 885 1754

Green Fee: ③   18 Holes   6818 yds   SSS: 73
Visitors: Anyday   Designer: John Harris
Tree-lined parkland course

Rouken Glen (1922)

Stewarton Road, Thornliebank, Glasgow G46 7UZ
Tel: 0141 638 7044
Green Fee: ①   18 Holes   5000 yds   SSS: 64
Visitors: Anyday   Designer: Unknown
Public parkland course

Sandyhills (1905)

223 Sandyhills Road, Sandyhills, Glasgow G32 9NA
Tel: 0141 778 1179
Green Fee: ①   18 Holes   6253 yds   SSS: 71
Visitors: Weekdays   Designer: Unknown
Parkland course

Whitecraigs (1905)

72 Ayr Road, Giffnock, Glasgow G46 6SW
Tel: 0141 639 4530   Fax: 0141 639 4530   Pro: 0141 639 2140
Green Fee: ③   18 Holes   6013 yds   SSS: 70
Visitors: Anyday   Designer: Unknown
Pleasant parkland course

Williamwood (1906)

Clarkston Road, Netherlee, Glasgow G44 3YR
Tel: 0141 637 1783   Fax: 0141 571 0166   Pro: 0141 637 2715
Green Fee: ②   18 Holes   5878 yds   SSS: 69
Visitors: Weekdays   Designer: James Braid
Undulating wooded parkland course

Windyhill (1908)

Baljaffray Road, Bearsden, Glasgow G61 4QQ
Tel: 0141 942 2349   Fax: 0141 942 5874   Pro: 0141 942 7157
Green Fee: ②   18 Holes   6254 yds   SSS: 70
Visitors: Weekdays   Designer: James Braid
Mixture of moor and parkland with panoramic views of the city

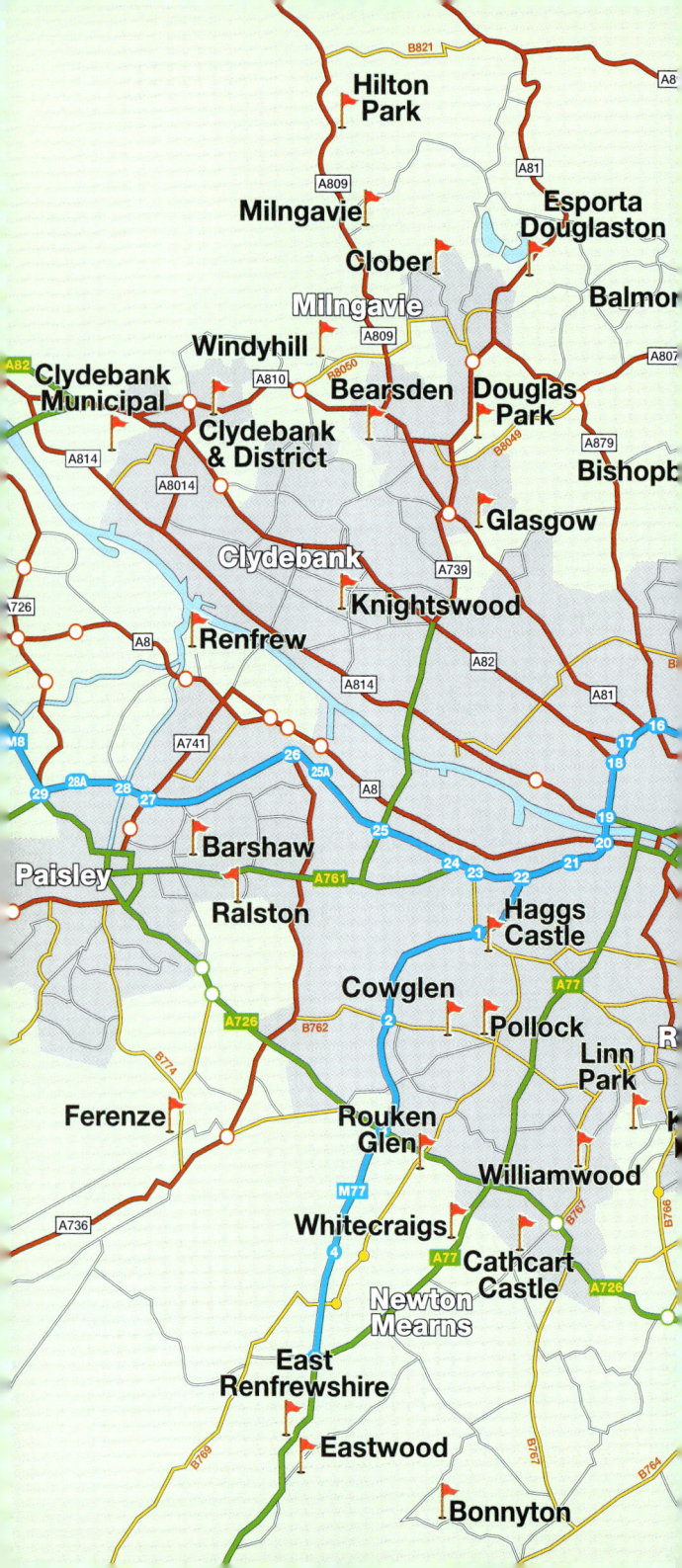

Hilton Park

B821

A8

A81

A809

Milngavie

Esporta Douglaston

Clober

Balmor

Milngavie

Windyhill

A809

A807

Clydebank Municipal

A82

A810

B8050

Bearsden

Douglas Park

A879

B8049

Bishopb

Clydebank & District

A814

A8014

Glasgow

Clydebank

A739

Knightswood

A726

A8

Renfrew

A814

A82

A81

M8

A741

26

25A

A8

17 16

18

29 28A 28 27

Barshaw

25

24 23 22 21

19

20

Paisley

A761

Ralston

1

Haggs Castle

Cowglen

A77

2

Pollock

Linn Park

R

B762

B774

A726

Ferenze

B762

Rouken Glen

Williamwood

A736

M77

Whitecraigs

4

B767

Cathcart Castle

A77

A726

B766

Newton Mearns

East Renfrewshire

B769

Eastwood

B767

B764

Bonnyton

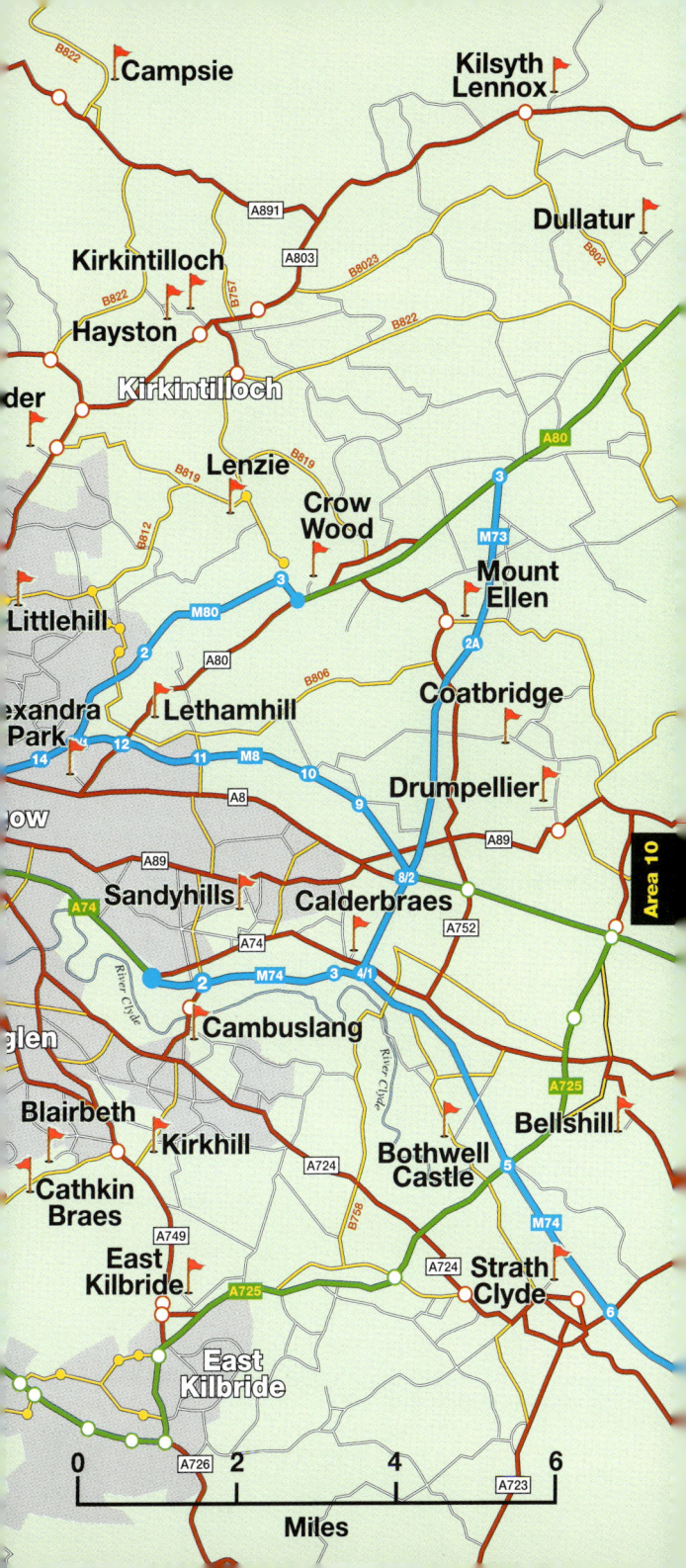

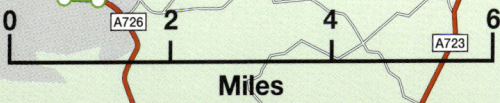

Campsie

Kilsyth
Lennox

Dullatur

B822

A891

Kirkintilloch

A803

B8023

B802

B822

B757

Hayston

B822

der

Kirkintilloch

Lenzie

B819

B819

Crow
Wood

A80

3

Littlehill

B812

M80

3

M73

Mount
Ellen

exandra
Park

2

A80

Lethamhill

B806

2A

Coatbridge

14

12

11

M8

10

9

Drumpellier

ow

A8

A89

A89

Area 10

A89

Sandyhills

Calderbraes

8/2

A74

A74

A752

River Clyde

2

M74

3

4/1

glen

Cambuslang

A725

Bellshill

Blairbeth

Kirkhill

River Clyde

Bothwell
Castle

5

Cathkin
Braes

A724

M74

A749

B758

East
Kilbride

A725

A724

Strath
Clyde

6

East
Kilbride

0   2   4   6

A726

A723

Miles

Area Eleven

Airdrie (1877)

Rochsoles, Airdrie, Lanarkshire ML6 0PQ
Tel: 01236 762195   Pro: 01236 754360
Green Fee: ①   18 Holes   6004 yds   SSS: 69
Visitors: Anyday   Designer: James Braid
Parkland course with pleasant views

Bathgate (1892)

Edinburgh Road, Bathgate, West Lothian EH48 1BA
Tel: 01506 652232 Fax: 01506 636775 Pro: 01506 630553

Green Fee: ①   18 Holes   6328 yds   SSS: 70
Visitors: Anyday   Designer: Willie Park
Parkland course

Bellshill (1905)

Community Road, Orbiston, Bellshill, Lanarkshire ML4 2RZ
Tel: 01698 745124   Fax: 01698 292576
Green Fee: ②   18 Holes   5850 yds   SSS: 69
Visitors: Anyday   Designer: Unknown
Parkland course, part moorland

Bonnybridge (1924)

Larbert Road, Bonnybridge, Falkirk, Stirlingshire FK4 1NY
Tel: 01324 812822
Green Fee: ①   9 Holes   6132 yds   SSS: 70
Visitors: Anyday   Designer: Unknown
Undulating moorland course

Colville Park (1923)

Jerviston Estate, Merry Street, Motherwell, Lanarkshire ML1 4UG
Tel: 01698 263017   Fax: 01698 230418   Pro: 01698 265779
Green Fee: ①   18 Holes   6303 yds   SSS: 70
Visitors: Weekdays   Designer: James Braid
Part tree-lined parkland course

Dalziel Park (1997)

Hagen Drive, Motherwell, Lanarkshire ML1 5RZ
Tel: 01698 862862   Fax: 01698 862863
Green Fee: ②   18 Holes   6200 yds   SSS: 70
Visitors: Anyday   Designer: Nigel Williams
Undulating parkland course

Deer Park (1978)

Golf Course Road, Livingston, West Lothian EH54 8AB
Tel: 01506 431037 or 446699   Fax: 01506 435608

Green Fee: ②   18 Holes   6688 yds   SSS: 72
Visitors: Anyday   Designers: Charles Lawrie/Alliss Thomas
Fairly flat parkland course

Dullatur (1896)

Glen Douglas Drive, Dullatur, Glasgow G68 0DW
Tel: 01236 723230   Fax: 01236 727271
Green Fee: ②   Antonine   18 Holes   5875 yds   SSS: 68
             ②   Carrickstone   18 Holes   6312 yds   SSS: 70
Visitors: Anyday   Designers: James Braid/Dave Thomas
Parkland course

Dundas Park (1957)

Dundas Estate, South Queensferry, Edinburgh EH30 9SS
Tel: 0131 331 5603 or 319 1347   Fax: 0131 319 1347
Green Fee: ①   9 Holes   6029 yds   SSS: 70
Visitors: Weekdays   Designer: Unknown
Parkland course within estate of Dundas Castle. Fine views

Easter Moffat (1922)

Station Road, Plains by Airdrie, Lanarkshire ML6 8NP
Tel: 01236 842878   Fax: 01236 842904   Pro: 01236 843015
Green Fee: ②   18 Holes   6240 yds   SSS: 70
Visitors: Weekdays   Designer: Unknown
Moorland/parkland course

Falkirk (1922)

136 Stirling Road, Camelon, Falkirk, Stirlingshire FK2 7YP
Tel: 01324 611061 Fax: 01324 639573 Pro: 01324 612219
Green Fee: ①   18 Holes   6282 yds   SSS: 70
Visitors: Anyday   Designer: James Braid
Parkland course with streams and gorse

Falkirk Tryst (1885)

86 Burnhead Road, Larbert, Stirlingshire FK5 4BD
Tel: 01324 562054 Fax: 01324 562054 Pro: 01324 562091

Green Fee: ②   18 Holes   6053 yds   SSS: 69
Visitors: Anyday   Designer: Unknown
Well-bunkered links-type course with trees and broom

Glenbervie (1932)

Stirling Road, Larbert, Stirlingshire FK5 4SJ
Tel: 01324 562605 Fax: 01324 551054 Pro: 01324 562725

Green Fee: ③   18 Holes   6423 yds   SSS: 71
Visitors: Weekdays   Designer: James Braid
Parkland course with pleasant views

Grangemouth (1973)

Polmonthill, by Falkirk, Stirlingshire FK2 0YA
Tel: 01324 711500 Fax: 01324 717907 Pro: 01324 503840
Green Fee: ①   18 Holes   6339 yds   SSS: 70
Visitors: Anyday   Designer: Sportwork
Public parkland course

Greenburn (1953)

6 Greenburn Road, Fauldhouse EH47 9AY
Tel: 01501 770292 Fax: 01501 772615 Pro: 01501 771187
Green Fee: ①   18 Holes   6210 yds   SSS: 71
Visitors: Anyday   Designer: Unknown
Moorland/parkland course

Harburn (1921)

West Calder, West Lothian EH55 8RS
Tel: 01506 871256 Fax: 01506 870286 Pro: 01506 871582
Green Fee: ②   18 Holes   5921 yds   SSS: 69
Visitors: Anyday   Designer: Unknown
Flat moorland/parkland course

Linlithgow (1913)

Breahead, Linlithgow, West Lothian EH49 6QF
Tel: 01506 842585 Fax: 01506 842764 Pro: 01506 844356

Green Fee: ②   18 Holes   5729 yds   SSS: 68
Visitors: Anyday except Saturday   Designer: Robert Simpson
Pleasant undulating parkland course

Niddry Castle (1983)

Castle Road, Winchburgh, West Lothian EH52 6RQ
Tel: 01506 891097 Fax: 01506 891097
Green Fee: ①   9 Holes   5518 yds   SSS: 67
Visitors: Anyday   Designer: Derek Smith
Parkland course

Oatridge (2000)

Ecclesmachan, Broxburn, West Lothian EH52 6NH
Tel: 01506 859636
Green Fee: ①   9 Holes   5962 yds   SSS: 71
Visitors: Anyday   Designer: Steve Marnoch
Parkland course with views to Binnycraig, an extinct volcano

Palacerigg (1975)

Palacerigg Country Park, Cumbernauld, Dumbartonshire G67 3HU
Tel: 01236 734969   Fax: 01236 721461   Pro: 01236 721461
Green Fee: ①   18 Holes   6444 yds   SSS: 71
Visitors: Anyday   Designer: Sir Henry Cotton
Well-wooded undulating public parkland course

Polkemmet (1981)

East Main Street, Whitburn, Bathgate, Midlothian EH47 0AD
Tel: 01501 743905
Green Fee: ①   9 Holes   6531 yds   SSS: 73
Visitors: Anyday   Designer: West Lothian District Council
Public parkland course

Polmont (1901)

Manuelrigg, Maddiston, by Falkirk, Stirlingshire FK2 0LS
Tel: 01324 711277   Fax: 01324 712504   Sec: 01324 713811

Green Fee: ①   9 Holes   6088 yds   SSS: 69
Visitors: Weekdays   Designer: Unknown
Undulating parkland course with pleasant views

Pumpherston (1895)

Drumshoreland Road, Pumpherston, West Lothian EH53 0LF
Tel: 01506 432869 or 433338

Green Fee: ②   18 Holes   6022 yds   SSS: 69
Visitors: Weekdays   Designer: Unknown
Undulating parkland course with views

Shotts (1895)

Benhar Road, Blairhead Shotts, Lanarkshire ML7 5BJ
Tel: 01501 820431 Pro: 01501 822658
Green Fee: ①   18 Holes   6205 yds   SSS: 70
Visitors: Anyday   Designer: James Braid
Hilly parkland/moorland course with panoramic views

Uphall (1895)

Houston Mains, Uphall, West Lothian EH52 6JT
Tel: 01506 856404 Fax: 01506 855358   Pro: 01506 855553

Green Fee: ①   18 Holes   5592 yds   SSS: 67
Visitors: Anyday   Designer: Unknown
Tree-lined parkland course

Westerwood Hotel (1989)

1 St. Andrews Drive, Cumbernauld, Dumbartonshire G68 0EW
Tel: 01236 457171   Fax: 01236 738478   Pro: 01236 725281

Green Fee: ③   18 Holes   6616 yds   SSS: 72
Visitors: Anyday   Designers: Seve Ballesteros and D. Thomas
Excellent undulating parkland course with silver birch and heather

West Lothian (1892)
Airngath Hill, Linlithgow, West Lothian EH49 7RH
Tel: 01506 826030   Fax: 01506 826462   Pro: 01506 825060
Green Fee: ②   18 Holes   6249 yds   SSS: 71
Visitors: Anyday
Designers: W. Park 1892/J. Adams 1923/F. Middleton 1975
Parkland course with wonderful views of the River Forth

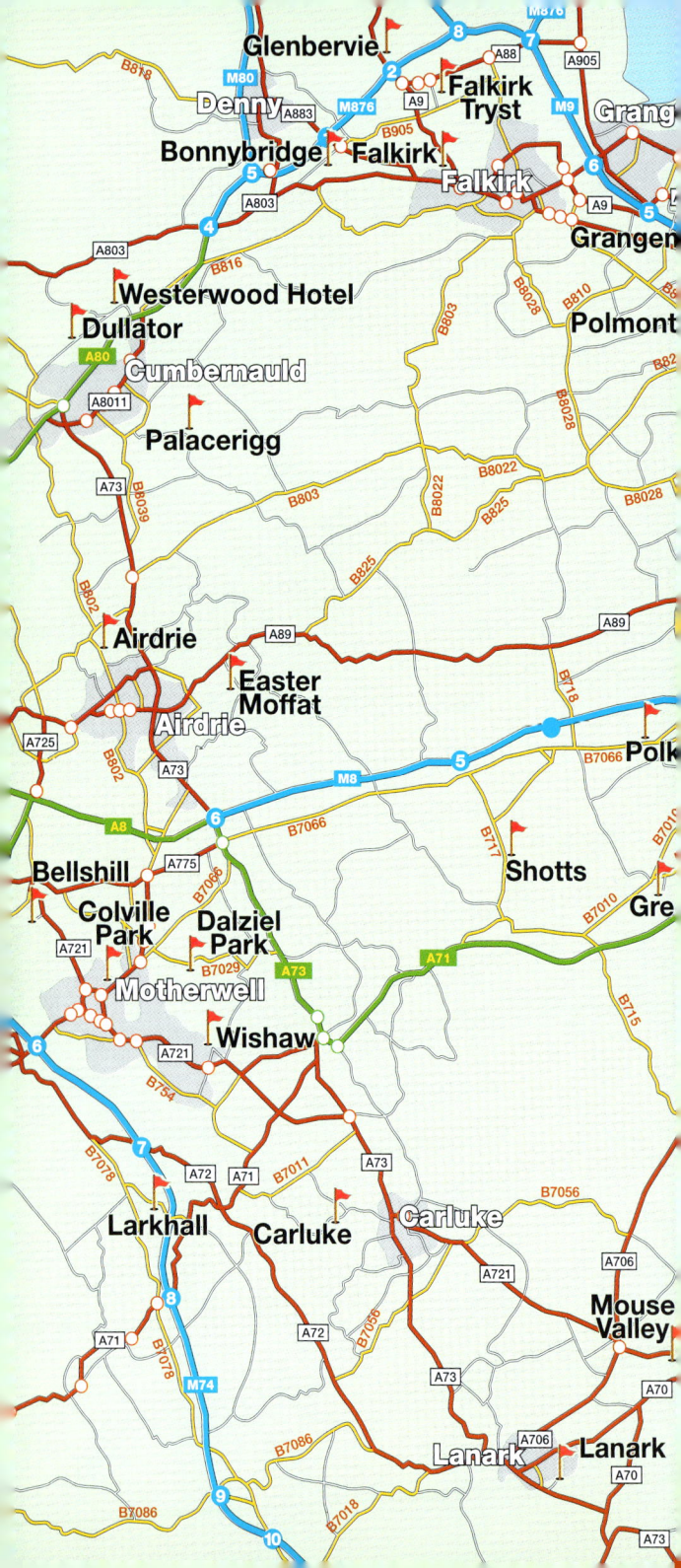

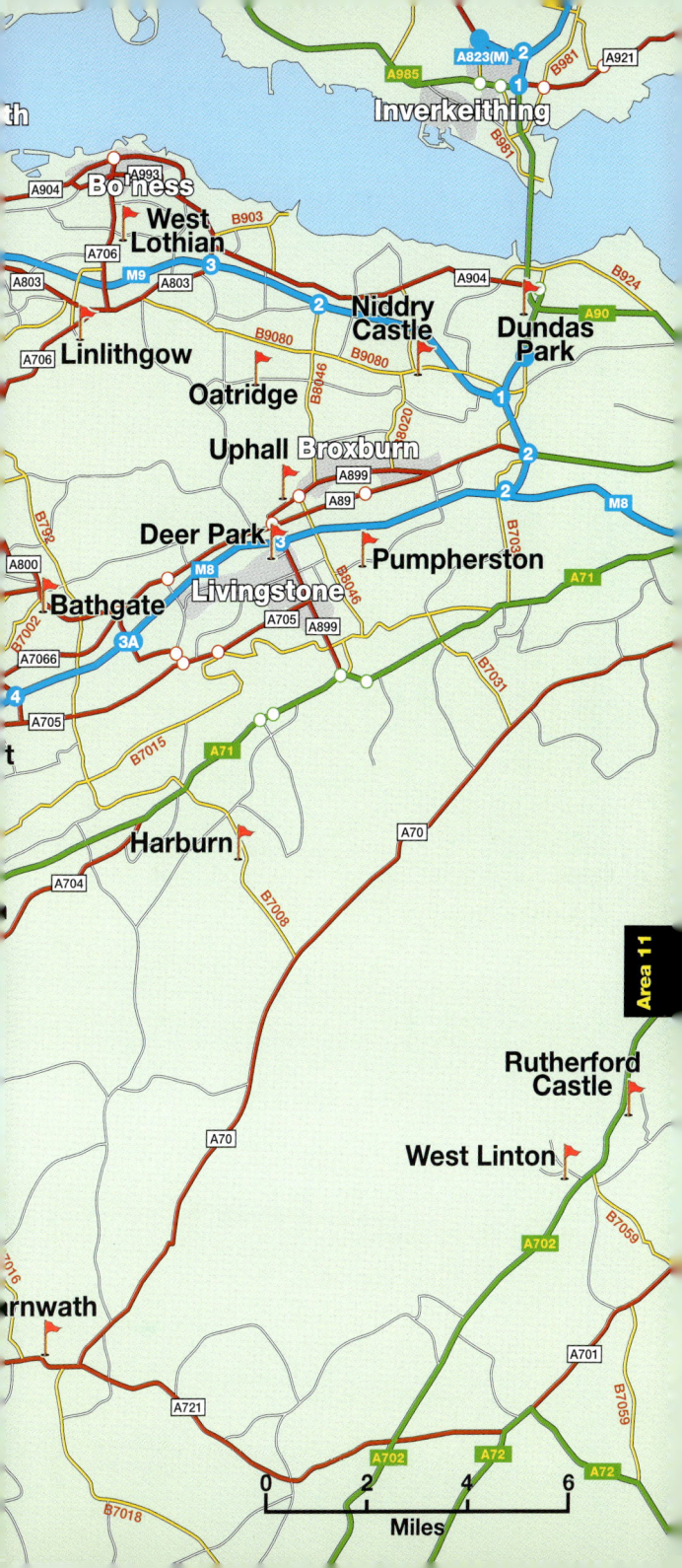

Inverkeithing

A823(M)

A985

B981

A921

B981

Bo'ness

A993

A904

West Lothian

B903

A706

M9

A803

A803

A803

Niddry Castle

A904

Dundas Park

A90

B924

Linlithgow

A706

B9080

Oatridge

B9080

B8046

Uphall

Broxburn

B9020

A899

A89

2

2

M8

Deer Park

3

Livingstone

Pumpherston

B8046

A703

A71

M8

Bathgate

B7002

A800

B792

A705

A899

A71

B7031

A7066

3A

4

A705

B7015

B7008

Harburn

A70

A704

A70

Rutherford Castle

West Linton

B7059

A702

A701

B7059

...arnwath

B7016

A721

B7018

A702

A72

A702

A72

0   2   4   6

Miles

Area Twelve

Baberton (1893)

50 Baberton Avenue, Juniper Green, Edinburgh EH14 5DU
Tel: 0131 453 4911   Fax: 0131 453 4678   Pro: 0131 453 3555
Green Fee: ②   18 Holes   6129 yds   SSS: 70
Visitors: Anyday   Designer: Willie Park
Parkland course

Braid Hills (1893)

Braid Hills Approach Road, Edinburgh EH10 6JY
Tel: 0131 452 9408   Fax: 0131 445 2044   Pro: 0131 447 6666

Green Fee: ①   18 Holes   5865 yds   SSS: 68
                    ①   18 Holes   4832 yds   SSS: 63
Visitors: Anyday   Designers: Peter McEwan & Bob Ferguson
Hilly heathland course with panoramic views and lots of gorse bushes

Broomieknowe (1906)

36 Golf Course Road, Bonnyrigg, Midlothian EH19 2HZ
Tel: 0131 663 9317   Fax: 0131 663 2152   Pro: 0131 660 2035
Green Fee: ①   18 Holes   6150 yds   SSS: 70
Visitors: Anyday   Designers: James Braid, alt. by Hawtree/B. Sayer
Mature parkland course with views

Bruntsfield Links (1761)

32 Barnton Avenue, Edinburgh EH4 6JH
Tel: 0131 336 1479   Fax: 0131 336 5538   Pro: 0131 336 4050
Green Fee: ③   18 Holes   6407 yds   SSS: 71
Visitors: Anyday
Designers: Willie Park/Mackenzie 1922/Hawtree 1974
Mature parkland course with excellent views

Carrick Knowe (1933)

Glendevon Park, Edinburgh EH12 5UZ
Tel: 0131 337 1096   Fax: 0131 337 2217
Green Fee: ①   18 Holes   6299 yds   SSS: 68
Visitors: Anyday   Designer: Unknown
Flat parkland course

Craigentinny (1891)

Craigentinny Avenue, Edinburgh EH7 6RG
Tel: 0131 554 7501

Green Fee: ①   18 Holes   5418 yds   SSS: 66
Visitors: Anyday   Designer: Unknown
Flat links course with "Arthur Scot's Seat" dominating the skyline

Craigielaw (2000)

Aberlady, East Lothian EH32 0PY
Tel: 01875 870800   Fax: 01875 870620
Green Fee: ③   18 Holes   6601 yds   SSS: 71
Visitors: Anyday   Designer: Unknown
Wonderful new links course overlooking Aberlady Bay. Lots of wildlife

Craigmillar Park (1895)

1 Observatory Road, Edinburgh EH9 3HG
Tel: 0131 667 0047   Pro: 0131 667 2850
Green Fee: ②   18 Holes   5851 yds   SSS: 69
Visitors: Weekdays   Designer: James Braid
Parkland course with panoramic views over the city

Duddingston (1895)

Duddingston Road West, Edinburgh EH15 3QD
Tel: 0131 661 7688   Fax: 0131 652 6057   Pro: 0131 661 4301

Area 12

Green Fee: ③   18 Holes   6473 yds   SSS: 72
Visitors: Weekdays   Designer: Willie Park
Parkland course with a burn running through

Glencorse (1890)
Milton Bridge, Pencuik, Midlothian EH26 0RD
Tel: 01968 677189   Fax: 01968 674399   Pro: 01968 676481

Green Fee: ②   18 Holes   5217 yds   SSS: 66
Visitors: Anyday   Designer: Willie Park
Parkland course with stream running through and in play at 10 holes

Gogarburn (1975)
Hanley Lodge, Newbridge, Midlothian EH28 8NN
Tel: 0131 333 4718 or 4110
Green Fee: ①   12 Holes   5070 yds   SSS: 64
Visitors: Anyday   Designer: Club Members
Parkland course

Kilspindie (1867)
Aberlady, Longniddry, East Lothian EH32 0QD
Tel: 01875 870358   Fax: 01875 870358   Pro: 01875 870695

Green Fee: ②   18 Holes   5480 yds   SSS: 66
Visitors: Anyday
Designers: Tom Morris, redesigned by Willie Park
Traditional seaside course on shores of River Forth

Kings Acre (1997)
Lasswade, Edinburgh EH18 1AU
Tel: 0131 663 3456   Fax: 0131 663 7076
Green Fee: ①   18 Holes   5935 yds   SSS: 68
Visitors: Anyday   Designer: Graeme Webster
Parkland course set in picturesque countryside

Kingsknowe (1908)

326 Lanark Road, Edinburgh EH14 2JD
Tel: 0131 441 1145   Fax: 0131 441 2079   Pro: 0131 441 4030
Green Fee: ②   18 Holes   5981 yds   SSS: 69
Visitors: Anyday   Designers: James Braid/Alex Herd/J. Stutt
Hilly parkland course

Liberton (1920)

297 Glimerton Road, Edinburgh EH16 5UJ
Tel: 0131 664 3009   Fax: 0131 666 0853   Pro: 0131 664 1056

Green Fee: ②   18 Holes   5306 yds   SSS: 66
Visitors: Anyday   Designer: Unknown
Parkland course

Longniddry (1921)

Links Road, Longniddry, East Lothian EH32 0NL
Tel: 01875 852141   Fax: 01875 853371   Pro: 01875 852228
Green Fee: ③   18 Holes   6260 yds   SSS: 70
Visitors: Anyday   Designer: Harry S. Colt
Undulating part links, part parkland course

Lothianburn (1893)

106a Biggar Road, Fairmilehead, Edinburgh EH10 7DU
Tel: 0131 445 5067 or 2206   Pro: 0131 445 2288

Green Fee: ①   18 Holes   5662 yds   SSS: 68
Visitors: Anyday   Designer: James Braid 1928
Hilly course with views of Edinburgh

Luffness New (1894)

Aberlady, East Lothian EH32 0QA
Tel: 01620 843114   Fax: 01620 843336
Green Fee: ③   18 Holes   6122 yds   SSS: 70
Visitors: Weekdays   Designer: Tom Morris
Links course used for Open Qualifying

Marriott Dalmahoy (1927)

Kirknewton, Midlothian EH27 8EB
Tel: 0131 335 8010   Fax: 0131 335 3203
Green Fee: ④   East   18 Holes   6677 yds   SSS: 72
　　　　　　③   West   18 Holes   5185 yds   SSS: 66
Visitors: Anyday   Designer: James Braid
Rolling parkland courses which have staged the Solheim Cup

Melville (1995)

South Melville, Lasswade, Midlothian EH18 1AN
Tel: 0131 654 0224   Fax: 0131 654 0814

Green Fee: ①   9 Holes   4604 yds   SSS: 62
Visitors: Anyday   Designer: Graeme Webster
Parkland course

Merchants of Edinburgh (1907)

10 Craighill Gardens, Morningside, Edinburgh EH10 5PY
Tel: 0131 447 1219   Fax: 0131 447 8709
Green Fee: ①   18 Holes   4889 yds   SSS: 64
Visitors: Weekdays   Designer: R. G. Ross
Hilly parkland course offering views over the city

Mortonhall (1892)

231 Braid Road, Edinburgh EH10 6PB
Tel: 0131 447 6974   Fax: 0131 447 8712   Pro: 0131 447 5185
Green Fee: ③   18 Holes   6557 yds   SSS: 72
Visitors: Anyday   Designer: James Braid/Fred Hawtree
Moorland/parkland course with views of Edinburgh

Murrayfield (1896)

43 Murrayfield Road, Edinburgh EH12 6EU
Tel: 0131 337 3478   Fax: 0131 313 0721   Pro: 0131 337 3479
Green Fee: ③   18 Holes   5765 yds   SSS: 69
Visitors: Weekdays   Designer: Unknown
Parkland course with views

Musselburgh (1938)

Monktonhall, Musselburgh, East Lothian EH21 6SA
Tel: 0131 665 2005   Pro: 0131 665 7055
Green Fee: ②   18 Holes   6725 yds   SSS: 73
Visitors: Anyday   Designer: James Braid
Difficult parkland course with natural hazards

Musselburgh Old (1672)

10 Balcarres Road, Musselburgh, East Lothian EH21 7SB
Tel: 0131 665 6981 or 5438   Fax: 0131 665 5438

Green Fee: ①   9 Holes   5774 yds   SSS: 69
Visitors: Anyday   Designer: Unknown
Seaside links course steeped in history with play within the race course

Newbattle (1896)

Abbey Road, Dalkeith, Midlothian EH22 3AD
Tel: 0131 663 1819   Fax: 0131 654 1810   Pro: 0131 660 1631
Green Fee: ②   18 Holes   6025 yds   SSS: 70
Visitors: Weekdays   Designer: Harry S. Colt
Undulating parkland course on different levels

Portobello (1826)

Stanley Street, Portobello, Edinburgh EH15 1JJ
Tel: 0131 669 4361 or 258 5028

Green Fee: ①   9 Holes   4504 yds   SSS: 64
Visitors: Weekdays   Designer: Unknown
Public parkland course

Prestonfield (1920)

6 Prestonfield Road North, Edinburgh EH16 5HS
Tel: 0131 667 9665   Fax: 0131 667 9665   Pro: 0131 667 8597
Green Fee: ②   18 Holes   6214 yds   SSS: 70
Visitors: Anyday   Designer: Peter Robertson
Parkland course with beautiful views

Ratho Park (1928)

Ratho, Newbridge, Edinburgh EH28 8NX
Tel: 0131 335 0069   Fax: 0131 333 1752   Pro: 0131 333 1406
Green Fee: ②   18 Holes   5932 yds   SSS: 68
Visitors: Anyday   Designer: James Braid
Flat parkland course

Ravelston (1912)

24 Ravelston Dykes Road, Blackhall, Edinburgh EH4 5NZ
Tel: 0131 315 2486   Fax: 0131 315 2486
Green Fee: ①   9 Holes   5218 yds   SSS: 65
Visitors: Weekdays   Designer: James Braid
Parkland course

Royal Burgess (1735)

181 Whitehouse Road, Barnton, Edinburgh EH4 6BY
Tel: 0131 339 2075   Fax: 0131 339 3712   Pro: 0131 339 6474
Green Fee: ③   18 Holes   6494 yds   SSS: 71
Visitors: Anyday   Designer: Tom Morris 1895/J. Braid 1945
Parkland course. Historic club – the oldest in the world

Royal Musselburgh (1774)

Prestongrange House, Prestonpans, East Lothian EH32 9RP
Tel: 01875 810276   Fax: 01875 810276   Pro: 01875 810139

Green Fee: ②   18 Holes   6237 yds   SSS: 70
Visitors: Anyday   Designer: James Braid
Challenging tree-lined parkland course by Firth of Forth

Silverknowes (1947)

11 Parkway, Silverknowes, Edinburgh EH4 5ET
Tel: 0131 336 3843   Fax: 0131 557 5170
Green Fee: ①   18 Holes   6097 yds   SSS: 70
Visitors: Anyday   Designer: Unknown
Public links course with magnificent views

Swanston (1927)

Swanston Road, Fairmilehead, Edinburgh EH10 7DS
Tel: 0131 445 2239 Fax: 0131 445 2239 Pro: 0131 445 4002

Green Fee: ① 18 Holes 5004 yds SSS: 65
Visitors: Anyday Designer: Herbert Moore
Hillside course

Torphin Hill (1895)

Torphin Road, Colinton, Edinburgh EH13 0PG
Tel: 0131 441 1100 Fax: 0131 441 7166 Pro: 0131 441 4061

Green Fee: ① 18 Holes 5230 yds SSS: 66
Visitors: Anyday Designer: Unknown
Hillside heathland course with pleasant views

Turnhouse (1897)

154 Turnhouse Road, Corstorphine, Edinburgh EH12 0AD
Tel: 0131 339 1844 Fax: 0131 339 1844 Pro: 0131 339 7701
Green Fee: ② 18 Holes 6135 yds SSS: 70
Visitors: Weekdays Designer: Unknown
Hilly parkland/heathland course with good views

Vogrie (1990)

Vogrie Estate Country Park, Gorebridge, Midlothian EH23 4NU
Tel: 01875 821716
Green Fee: ① 9 Holes 5060 yds SSS: 66
Visitors: Anyday Designer: Unknown
Public parkland course situated within Country Park

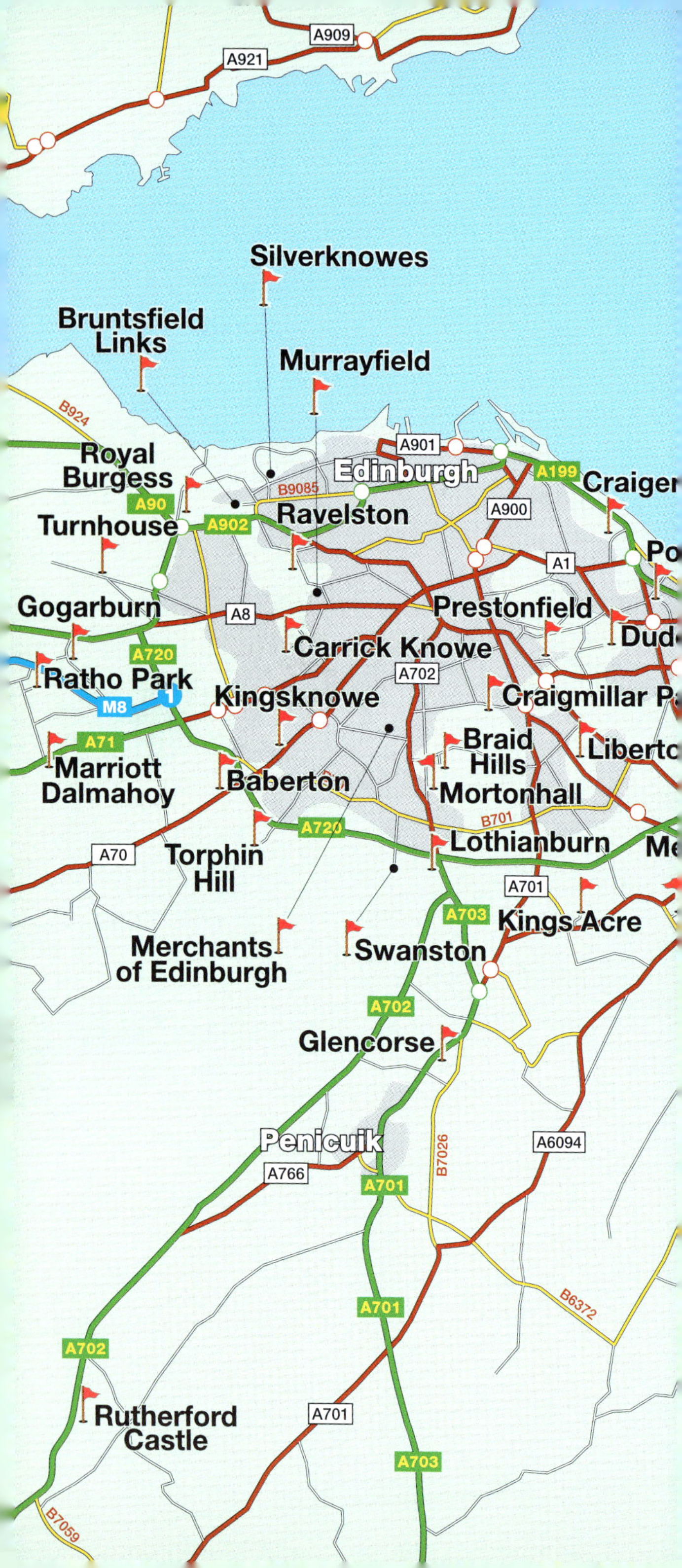

A909
A921
A924 B924

Silverknowes

Bruntsfield
Links

Murrayfield

Royal
Burgess
A90
Turnhouse A902 B9085 Edinburgh A199 Craiger
Ravelston
A901
A900
Gogarburn A8 A1 Po
Prestonfield
A720 Carrick Knowe Dud
Ratho Park A702
M8 1 Craigmillar P
Kingsknowe
A71 Braid Liberto
Marriott Hills
Dalmahoy Baberton Mortonhall
A720 Lothianburn Me
A70 B701
Torphin A701
Hill A703 Kings Acre
Merchants A702
of Edinburgh Swanston

Glencorse

A702

Penicuik
A766 A701
B7026 A6094

A701 B6372

A702
A701
Rutherford B7059 A703
Castle

Gullane

Luffness New

Kilspindie

Craigielaw

A198

Musselburgh
Old

Royal
Musselburgh

A198

Longniddry

B1377

A61

B1348

llo

ton

A1

Musselburgh

A199

A1

B6414

B6355

B6363

B6371

A6093

B6355

B6368

A6124

Newbattle

A68

B6371

nieknowe

B6648

Vogrie

B6367

B645

A7

B6372

B6458

B6368

B7007

A7

A68

Area 12

0   2   4   6

Miles

B709

Annanhill (1957)

Irvine Road, Kilmarnock, Ayrshire KA1 2RT
Tel: 01563 521512 or 521644
Green Fee: ①   18 Holes   6198 yds   SSS: 69
Visitors: Anyday   Designer: John McLean
Pay and play, tree-lined, undulating parkland course

Ardeer (1880)

Greenhead Avenue, Stevenston, Ayrshire KA20 4JX
Tel: 01294 464542   Fax: 01294 465316   Pro: 01294 601327
Green Fee: ②   18 Holes   6409 yds   SSS: 72
Visitors: Weekdays   Designer: W. Stutt
Parkland course with natural water hazards

Auchenharvie (1981)

Moor Park Road, Stevenson, Ayrshire KA20 3HU
Tel: 01294 603775   Pro: 01294 603103
Green Fee: ①   9 Holes   5203 yds   SSS: 65
Visitors: Anyday   Designers: Mitchell/Struthers
Pay and play part parkland/links course

Ballochmyle (1937)

Ballochmyle, Mauchline, Ayrshire KA5 6LE
Tel: 01290 550469   Fax: 01290 553657
Green Fee: ②   18 Holes   5972 yds   SSS: 69
Visitors: Anyday   Designer: Unknown
Pretty wooded and challenging parkland course

Belleisle (1927)

Doonfoot Road, Ayr, Ayrshire KA7 4DU
Tel: 01292 441258   Fax: 01292 441632   Pro: 01292 441314

Green Fee: ②   18 Holes   6431 yds   SSS: 72
Visitors: Anyday   Designer: James Braid
Pay to play parkland course. Regarded as one of the best public layouts in Scotland.
Fairways flanked by hundreds of beech trees and crossed by winding burn

Brodick (1897)

Brodick, Isle of Arran, Ayrshire KA27 8DL
Tel: 01770 302349   Fax: 01770 302349   Pro: 01770 302513

Green Fee: ②   18 Holes   4736 yds   SSS: 64
Visitors: Anyday   Designer: Unknown
Flat course alongside the Firth of Clyde with very pleasant views

Brunston Castle (1992)

Dailly, Girvan, Ayrshire KA26 9RH
Tel: 01465 811471   Fax: 01465 811545
Green Fee: ②   18 Holes   6662 yds   SSS: 72
Visitors: Anyday   Designer: Donald Steel
Sheltered inland parkland course. River Girvan runs through the course

Caprington (1907)

Ayr Road, Kilmarnock, Ayrshire KA1 4UW
Tel: 01563 521915 or 523702   Fax: 01563 523702
Green Fee: ①   18 Holes   5748 yds   SSS: 68
Visitors: Anyday   Designer: Unknown
Pay and play parkland course

Corrie (1892)

Corrie, Sannox, Isle of Arran, Ayrshire KA27 8JD
Tel: 01770 810223 or 810606

Green Fee: ①   9 Holes   3896 yds   SSS: 61
Visitors: Anyday   Designer: Unknown
Short fairly hilly course with marvellous views. Although only 9 holes, this course is extremely interesting and very picturesque

Dalmilling (1961)

Westwood Avenue, Ayr, Ayrshire KA8 0QU
Tel: 01292 263893 or 267651   Fax: 01292 610543
Green Fee: ① 18 Holes 5724 yds SSS: 68
Visitors: Anyday   Designer: Unknown
Easy walking meadowland course

Doon Valley (1927)

Hillside, Patna, Ayrshire KA6 7JT
Tel: 01292 531607 Fax: 01292 532489
Green Fee: ① 9 Holes 5886 yds SSS: 68
Visitors: Weekdays   Designer: Unknown
Pay and play hillside moorland course

Girvan (1900)

Golf Course Road, Girvan, Ayrshire KA26 9HW
Tel: 01465 714346   Fax: 01465 714346
Green Fee: ① 18 Holes 5064 yds SSS: 64
Visitors: Anyday   Designer: James Braid
Pay and play seaside course with mixture of links (8 holes) and parkland (10 holes)

Glasgow Gailes (1892)

Gailes, Irvine, Ayrshire KA11 5AE
Tel: 01294 311258   Fax: 01294 279366   Pro: 01294 311561

Green Fee: ③ 18 Holes 6535 yds SSS: 72
Visitors: Anyday   Designer: Willie Park, Jnr.
Open Championship Qualifying links course situated alongside the railway adjacent to Western Gailes. A wonderful challenge

Irvine (1887)

Bogside, Irvine, Ayrshire KA12 8SN
Tel: 01294 275979   Fax: 01294 278209   Pro: 01294 275626
Green Fee: ③ 18 Holes 6408 yds SSS: 71
Visitors: Anyday   Designer: James Braid
Lovely testing links course also used for Open Qualifying with railway running alongside

Irvine Ravenspark (1907)

Kidsneuk Lane, Irvine, Ayrshire KA12 8SR
Tel: 01294 271293   Pro: 01294 276467
Green Fee: ① 18 Holes 6429 yds SSS: 71
Visitors: Anyday   Designer: Unknown
Pay and play parkland course

Kilmarnock Barassie (1887)

29 Hillhouse Road, Barassie, Ayrshire KA10 6SY
Tel: 01292 313920   Fax: 01292 318300   Pro: 01292 311322
Green Fee: ④   18 Holes   6484 yds   SSS: 73
Visitors: Mon/Tues/Thurs/Fri   Designer: Theodore Moone
Wonderful seaside links course used for Open Qualifying. Lots of heather and relatively flat

Lamlash (1889)

Lamlash, Isle of Arran, Ayrshire KA27 8JU
Tel: 01770 600296   Fax: 01770 600296
Green Fee: ①   18 Holes   4640 yds   SSS: 64
Visitors: Anyday   Designers: Willie Auchterlonie/Willie Fernie
Undulating heathland course with magnificent sea and mountain views

Lochranza (1991)

Lochranza, Isle of Arran, Ayrshire KA27 8HL
Tel: 01770 830273   Fax: 01770 830600
Green Fee: ①   18 Holes   5487 yds   SSS: 70
Visitors: Anyday   Designer: Iain Robertson
Set in a natural amphitheatre with red deer and eagles soaring overhead.
Water hazards on 12 holes. Closed November-March

Loudoun Gowf (1909)

Newmilns Road, Galston, Ayrshire KA4 8PA
Tel: 01563 820551 or 821993   Fax: 01563 820011

Green Fee: ②   18 Holes   6016 yds   SSS: 69
Visitors: Weekdays   Designer: Unknown
Testing parkland course with mature trees. Named on old maps as "Gowf
Fields of Loudoun" thus providing the unique spelling of the club

Machrie Bay (1900)

Machrie Bay, Machrie, Isle of Arran, Ayrshire KA27 8DZ
Tel: 01770 850232   Fax: 01770 850247
Green Fee: ①   9 Holes   4440 yds   SSS: 64
Visitors: Anyday   Designer: Willie Fernie
Flattish course running alongside the shore. Lovely views of the Mull of Kintyre

Maybole (1970)

Memorial Park, Maybole, Ayrshire KA19 7EB
Tel: 01292 612000
Green Fee: ①   9 Holes   5270 yds   SSS: 66
Visitors: Anyday   Designer: Unknown
Pay and play hilly parkland course. Beautiful setting with splendid views

Prestwick (1851)

2 Links Road, Prestwick, Ayrshire KA9 1QG
Tel: 01292 477404   Fax: 01292 477255   Pro: 01292 479483

Green Fee: (5)   18 Holes   6544 yds   SSS: 73
Visitors: Weekdays   Designer: Tom Morris

Home of the Open Championship. The first was played here in 1860, the last in 1925. From the 1st hole with the Railway wall on the right, this classic links course will test you all the way, but leave you with marvellous memories. Clubhouse contains a wide range of memorabilia

Prestwick St Cuthbert (1899)

East Road, Prestwick, Ayrshire KA9 2SX
Tel: 01292 477101   Fax: 01292 671730
Green Fee: (2)   18 Holes   6470 yds   SSS: 71
Visitors: Weekdays   Designer: Hamilton Stutt in 1960
Undulating parkland course with natural hazards

Prestwick St Nicholas (1851)

Grangemuir Road, Prestwick, Ayrshire KA9 1SN
Tel: 01292 477608 or 473904 Fax: 01292 473900

Green Fee: (3)   18 Holes   5952 yds   SSS: 69
Visitors: Not Sats   Designer: Charles Hunter

Challenging links course used for Open Qualifying. Pleasant views of the Isle of Arran

Royal Troon (1878)

Craigend Road, Troon, Ayrshire KA10 6EP
Tel: 01292 311555   Fax: 01292 318204   Pro: 01292 313281

Green Fee: ⑦ Royal Troon	18 Holes	7097 yds	SSS: 74
Visitors: Mon/Tues/Thurs	Designer: Willie Fernie		
Green Fee: ⑥ Portland	18 Holes	6289 yds	SSS: 71
Visitors: Weekdays	Designer: Unknown		

A links course set along the coast. This is indeed a
championship course. The "Open" has been held here on
occasions. Renowned for its 8th hole called the "Postage
Stamp" because of the small green. Greg Norman holds
the course record with a 64 but he dropped his only shot
on this hole. Although Portland is not the championship
course, it is not to be missed or taken lightly

Seafield (1930)

Doonfoot Road, Ayr, Ayrshire KA7 4DU
Tel: 01292 441258   Fax: 01292 442632   Pro: 01292 441314
Green Fee: ①   18 Holes   5246 yds   SSS: 67
Visitors: Anyday   Designer: Unknown
Situated in the Belleisle Park, this Pay and Play course offers an intriguing mixtures
of 10 parkland and 8 links type holes. Shares the Clubhouse with Belleisle

Shiskine (1896)

Blackwaterfoot, Isle of Arran, Ayrshire KA27 8HA
Tel: 01770 860226   Fax: 01770 860205
Green Fee: ①   12 Holes   2990 yds   SSS: 42 (64 for 18)
Visitors: Anyday   Designer: Unknown
Unique 12 hole links course with marvellous views of the Mull of Kintyre

Southern Gailes (2002)

Gailes Road, Irvine, Ayrshire KA11 5AU
Tel: 01294 311799 Fax: 01294 276473
Green Fee: (5)   18 Holes   7401 yds   SSS: 72
Visitors: Anyday   Designer: Kyle Phillips

Links course for the 21st century incorporating all the best features of Scottish golf – gorse, heather etc.

Troon Municipals (1905)

Harling Drive, Troon, Ayrshire KA10 6NE
Tel: 01292 312464   Fax: 01292 312578   Pro: 01292 315566

Green Fee:				
(1)	Darley	18 Holes	6501 yds	SSS: 72
(1)	Fullarton	18 Holes	4822 yds	SSS: 63
(2)	Lochgreen	18 Holes	6785 yds	SSS: 73

Visitors: Anyday   Designer: Gordon McKinlay

Darley: Links course offering a real challenge with hazards of heather, gorse and whin
Fullarton: This Pay and Play course is ideal for beginners, being the shortest of the three course. Has 8 par 3 holes
Lochgreen: Has in the past been used as a Qualifying course for the Open. The longest and most testing of the Troon Pay and Play courses

Turnberry (1906)

Turnberry Hotel, Turnberry, Ayrshire KA26 9LT
Tel: 01655 331000   Fax: 01655 331706

Green Fee:				
(6)	Ailsa	18 Holes	6976 yds	SSS: 72
(5)	Kintyre	18 Holes	6853 yds	SSS: 72

Visitors: Hotel residents only
Designers: Hutchinson/Mackenzie Ross

One of the world's great places to play. A truly championship links course where one of the greatest "Open Championships" took place in 1977. "The Duel in the Sun" with Tom Watson and Jack Nicklaus. To be playing golf here on a summer's evening with the Piper playing outside the hotel will leave you with a lifetime of memories

Western Gailes (1897)
Gailes, Irvine, Ayrshire KA11 5AE
Tel: 01294 311649   Fax: 01294 312312

Green Fee: (5)   18 Holes   6639 yds   SSS: 73
Visitors: Anyday   Designer: Tom Morris
A truly marvellous seaside links course. Used also for Open Qualifying. Should not be missed. Three burns criss cross the course. Impressive views of Arran and Ailsa Craig

West Kilbride (1893)
Fullarton Drive, West Kilbride, Ayrshire KA23 9HT
Tel: 01294 823911   Fax: 01294 829573   Pro: 01294 823042

Green Fee: (2)   18 Holes   6452 yds   SSS: 71
Visitors: Weekdays   Designer: Tom Morris
Traditional flat seaside links alongside Firth of Clyde. Pleasant course with views of the Isle of Arran

Whiting Bay (1895)
Golf Course Road, Whiting Bay, Isle of Arran, Ayrshire KA27 8PR
Tel: 01770 700487
Green Fee: (1)   18 Holes   4405 yds   SSS: 63
Visitors: Anyday   Designer: Unknown
Heathland course

B8001

B881

B898

B899

A844

Lochranza

A841

Corrie

Wes
Kilbri

Au
Glasgow G.
Souther
Western G

A r r a n

A841

Brodick

B880

A841

Machrie
Bay

Lamlash

Royal

Shiskine

Whiting
Bay

Prestwic

A841

Turnbe

Girva

0   2   4   6
Miles

Largs

Lochwinoch

Barrhead

M77

A760

A760

Kilbirnie

A736

B776

B775

Beith

Caldwell

B777

B777

B706

B769

B764

B781

B707

A737

B778

B780

B780

Ardeer

B778

B778

A77

A738

A78

A736

A735

B751

A719

Irvine Ravenspark

B769

oats

harvie

Irvine

A737

Irvine

Annanhill

Loudoun Gowf

A71

Kilmarnock

A71

B7080

A730

A759

Caprington

B730

es

narnock Barassie

B730

B751

A719

A76

B7031

Troon

B730

A78

A77

Mauchline

B743

B705

Troon Municipals

B739

B7036

Prestwick

Prestwick St. Cuthbert

Ballochmyle

licholas

Dalmilling

A79

afield

A79

Ayr

A713

A70

eisle

B742

A77

B742

A713

B7024

B742

B7036

B742

B7034

A713

Doon Valley

A719

B7046

B7023

B7023

Maybole

B7045

B741

A77

B741

B741

A713

B741

Brunston Castle

B734

Area 13

Area Fourteen

Arbory Brae (1892)

Coldchapel Road, Abington, South Lanarkshire ML12 6RW
Tel: 01555 664634

Green Fee: ①   9 Holes   3770 yds   SSS: 62
Visitors: Anyday   Designer: Willie Fernie

Closed in 1938. Course reconstructed in 2000 to appear as original

Biggar (1895)

The Park, Broughton, Lanarkshire ML12 6AH
Tel: 01899 220319 or 220618   Fax: 01899 221738

Green Fee: ①   18 Holes   5537 yds   SSS: 67
Visitors: Anyday   Designer: Willie Park

Pleasant, scenic public parkland course

Bonnyton (1957)

Kirktonmoor Road, Eaglesham, Glasgow G76 0QA
Tel: 01355 302781   Fax: 01355 303151   Pro: 01355 302256

Green Fee: ③   18 Holes   6252 yds   SSS: 71
Visitors: Weekdays   Designer: Unknown

Beautiful, scenic and challenging heather covered moorland course

Carluke (1894)

Hallcraig, Mauldslie Road, Carluke, Lanarkshire ML8 5HG
Tel: 01555 770574   Fax: 01555 770574   Pro: 01555 751053

Green Fee: ②   18 Holes   5899 yds   SSS: 69
Visitors: Weekdays   Designer: Unknown

Parkland course with views over Clydebank

Carnwath (1907)

1 Main Street, Carnwath, Strathclyde ML11 8JX
Tel: 01555 840251 or 840023   Fax: 01555 841070

Green Fee: ①   18 Holes   5955 yds   SSS: 69
Visitors: Anyday   Designer: Unknown

Panoramic views from this hilly parkland course

Douglas Water (1922)

Ayr Road, Rigside, Lanarkshire ML11 9NB
Tel: 01555 880361
Green Fee: ①   9 Holes   5832 yds   SSS: 69
Visitors: Anyday   Designers: Striking Coal Miners
Undulating parkland course offering spectacular views

Eastwood (1893)

Loganwell, Newton Mearns, Glasgow G77 6RX
Tel: 01355 500280 or 500261   Pro: 01355 500285
Green Fee: ②   18 Holes   5864 yds   SSS: 69
Visitors: Weekdays   Designer: Theodore Moone
Undulating moorland course

Hamilton (1892)

Ferniegair, Hamilton, Lanarkshire ML3 7UE
Tel: 01698 459537   Fax: 01698 459537   Pro: 01698 282324
Green Fee: ③   18 Holes   6264 yds   SSS: 71
Visitors: Weekdays   Designer: James Braid
Very pleasant parkland course

Hollandbush (1954)

Acre Tophead, Lesmahagow, Strathclyde ML11 0JS
Tel: 01555 893484   Fax: 01555 893484   Pro: 01555 893646
Green Fee: ①   18 Holes   6233 yds   SSS: 70
Visitors: Anyday   Designers: Ken Pate and J. Lawson
Fairly difficult tree-lined park and moorland public course

Lanark (1851)

The Moor, Whitelees Road, Lanark, Lanarkshire ML11 7RX
Tel: 01555 663219   Fax: 01555 663219   Pro: 01555 661456

Green Fee: ②   18 Holes   6306 yds   SSS: 71
Visitors: Anyday   Designers: Ben Sayers/James Braid
Moorland course with pleasant views

Langlands (1985)

Langlands Road, East Kilbride, Strathclyde G75 9DW
Tel: 01355 224685 or 248173   Fax: 01355 248121
Green Fee: ①   18 Holes   6202 yds   SSS: 70
Visitors: Anyday   Designer: Unknown
Flat parkland course with views of surrounding countryside

Larkhall (1909)
Burnhead Road, Larkhall, Lanarkshire ML9 3AA
Tel: 01698 881113 or 889597
Green Fee: ①   9 Holes   6423 yds   SSS: 71
Visitors: Anyday   Designer: Unknown
Public parkland course

Leadhills (1935)
Leadhills, Biggar, Lanarkshire ML12 6XT
Tel: 01659 74456

Green Fee: ①   9 Holes   4062 yds   SSS: 62
Visitors: Anyday   Designer: Unknown
Moorland course which is the highest in Scotland

Moffat (1884)
Coatshill, Moffat, Dumfriesshire DG10 9SB
Tel: 01683 220020   Fax: 01683 221802   Sec: 01683 220336
Green Fee: ②   18 Holes   5259 yds   SSS: 67
Visitors: Anyday   Designer: Ben Sayers
Lovely upland course overlooking the town with truly magnificent views

Mouse Valley (1993)
East End, Cleghorn, Lanarkshire ML11 8NR
Tel: 01555 870015   Fax: 01555 870022
Green Fee: ①   Valley   18 Holes   6680 yds   SSS: 72
         ①   Kames   9 Holes   5076 yds   SSS: 65
Visitors: Anyday   Designer: Graham Taylor
Undulating meadowland course with country views

Muirkirk (1991)
65 Main Street, Muirkirk, Ayrshire KA18 3QR
Tel: 01290 660184
Green Fee: ①   9 Holes   5366 yds   SSS: 67
Visitors: Anyday   Designer: Unknown
Moorland course with pleasant views of the Cairn Table (1900ft)

New Cumnock (1901)
Lochill, Cumnock Road, New Cumnock, Ayrshire KA18 4BQ
Tel: 01290 338041
Green Fee: ①   9 Holes   5176 yds   SSS: 65
Visitors: Weekdays   Designer: Willie Fernie
Hard-walking hillside course with fine views overlooking the Loch

Sanquhar (1894)

Blackaddie Road, Sanquhar, Dumfriesshire DG4 6JZ
Tel: 01659 50577

Green Fee: ①   9 Holes   5594 yds   SSS: 68
Visitors: Anyday   Designer: Willie Fernie
Parkland course with marvellous panoramic views of the Dee estuary

Strathaven (1908)

Overton Ave, Glasgow Road, Strathaven, Strathclyde ML10 6NL
Tel: 01357 520421   Fax: 01357 520539   Pro: 01357 521812

Green Fee: ②   18 Holes   6226 yds   SSS: 71
Visitors: Weekdays   Designers: Willie Fernie extended to 18 by J. R. Stutt
This undulating tree-lined parkland course offers fine views of the town

Strathclyde Park (1891)

Mote Hill, Hamilton, Lanarkshire ML3 6BY
Tel: 01698 429350

Green Fee: ①   9 Holes   6350 yds   SSS: 70
Visitors: Anyday   Designer: Unknown
Public parkland course

Thornhill (1893)

Blacknest, Thornhill, Dumfriesshire DG3 5DW
Tel: 01848 330546   Pro: 01848 331779

Green Fee: ①   18 Holes   6085 yds   SSS: 70
Visitors: Anyday   Designer: Willie Fernie
Mixture of park and heathland with wonderful scenery

Torrance House (1969)

Strathaven Road, East Kilbride, Strathclyde G75 0QZ
Tel: 01355 248638   Fax: 01355 233451   Pro: 01355 233451

Green Fee: ①   18 Holes   6400 yds   SSS: 71
Visitors: Weekdays   Designer: Hawtree & Son
Mature public parkland course

Wishaw (1897)

55 Cleland Road, Wishaw, Lanarkshire ML2 7PH
Tel: 01698 357480   Fax: 01698 357480   Pro: 01698 358247

Green Fee: ①   18 Holes   5999 yds   SSS: 69
Visitors: Anyday   Designer: James Braid
Parkland course

Area 14

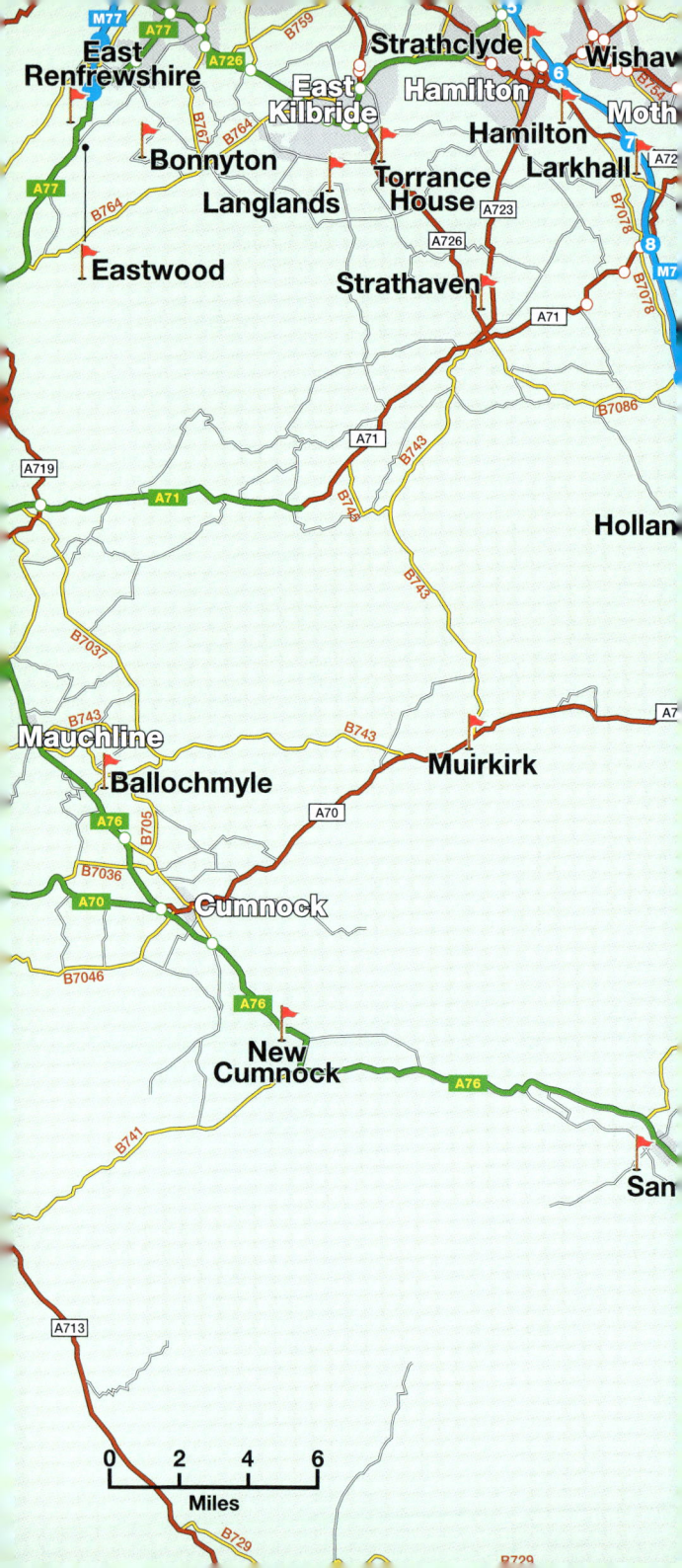

A71
B715
A73
B7056
A706
A70
A721
B7016
Carnwath
A70
B7056
A73
A706
Mouse Valley
A721
A70
A702
A72
Lanark
B7016
A70
A73
Biggar
B7016
A701
A72
B7078
11
Douglas Water
B7055
A73
A702
12
M74
B7078
13
Arbory Brae
A701
14
14
B797
B740
B7040
A702
B7078
Leadhills
B797
B719
A701
Moffat
Area 14
A702
A76
A702
15
M74
Thornhill
A701
B7020
B7078
A76
A702
16

Cardrona Hotel (2001)

Peebles, Peebleshire EH45 9HX
Tel: 01896 831971   Fax: 01896 831660
Green Fee: ②   18 Holes   6856 yds   SSS: 73
Visitors: Anyday   Designer: Dave Thomas
Parkland course set in beautiful countryside alongside River Tweed

Castle Park (1994)

Gifford, East Lothian EH41 4PL
Tel: 01620 810733   Fax: 01620 810733

Green Fee: ①   9 Holes   5744 yds   SSS: 68
Visitors: Anyday   Designers: Local Golfers
Public parkland course amongst mature woodlands

Dunbar (1856)

East Links, Dunbar, East Lothian EH42 1LL
Tel: 01368 862317   Fax: 01368 865202   Pro: 01368 862086
Green Fee: ③   18 Holes   6426 yds   SSS: 71
Visitors: Anyday   Designer: Tom Morris
Challenging course on narrow strip of land which follows the sea

Duns (1894)

Hardens Road, Duns, Berwickshire TD11 3NR
Tel: 01361 882717 or 882194
Green Fee: ①   18 Holes   6209 yds   SSS: 70
Visitors: Anyday   Designer: A. H. Scott
Upland course with burn running through. Pleasant views

Eyemouth (1894)

Gunsgreen Hill, Eyemouth, Berwickshire TD14 5SF
Tel: 01890 750551   Pro: 01890 750004
Green Fee: ②   18 Holes   6520 yds   SSS: 72
Visitors: Anyday   Designer: J. R. Bain
Clifftop seaside course with panoramic views of the village and sea

Galashields (1884)

Ladhope Recreation Ground, Galashields, Selkirkshire TD1 2DL
Tel: 01896 755307 or 753724

Green Fee: ①   18 Holes   5311 yds   SSS: 66
Visitors: Anyday   Designer: James Braid

Hilly hillside course with rewarding views

Gifford (1904)

Edinburgh Road, Gifford, East Lothian EH41 4JE
Tel: 01620 810591 or 810267

Green Fee: ①   9 Holes   6256 yds   SSS: 70
Visitors: Anyday   Designer: Willie Wood

Undulating parkland course

Glen (1894)

East Links, Tantallon, North Berwick, East Lothian EH39 4LE
Tel: 01620 892726   Fax: 01620 895447

Green Fee: ②   18 Holes   6079 yds   SSS: 69
Visitors: Anyday   Designers: James Braid/Ben Sayers/MacKenzie Ross

Seaside links with stunning views of the town and Bass Rock

Gullane (1882)

West Links Road, Gullane, East Lothian EH31 2BB
Tel: 01620 842255   Fax: 01620 842327   Pro: 01620 843111

Green Fee: ④   No. 1   18 Holes   6466 yds   SSS: 72
         ③   No. 2   18 Holes   6244 yds   SSS: 70
         ①   No. 3   18 Holes   5252 yds   SSS: 66
Visitors: Anyday   Designer: Willie Park

Seaside links courses with magnificent views of Gullane, also used for Open Qualifying

Haddington (1865)

Amisfield Park, Haddington, East Lothian EH41 4PT
Tel: 01620 823627   Fax: 01620 826580   Pro: 01620 822727

Green Fee: ②   18 Holes   6317 yds   SSS: 70
Visitors: Anyday   Designer: Unknown

Undulating parkland course in grounds of former country estate

Hawick (1877)

Vertish Hill, Hawick, Roxburghshire TD9 0NY
Tel: 01450 374947 or 372293

Green Fee: ②   18 Holes   5933 yds   SSS: 69
Visitors: Anyday   Designer: Unknown

Parkland course. Quite hilly with panoramic countryside views

Area 15

Hirsel (1948)

Kelso Road, Coldstream, Berwickshire TD12 4NJ
Tel: 01890 882678   Fax: 01890 882233   Sec: 01890 883052
Green Fee: ②   18 Holes   6111 yds   SSS: 70
Visitors: Anyday   Designer: Unknown
Beautiful parkland course set in Hirsel estate with panoramic views

Innerleithen (1886)

Leithen Water, Leithen Road, Innerleithen, Peebleshire EH44 6NL
Tel: 01896 830951 or 830071

Green Fee: ①   9 Holes   6066 yds   SSS: 69
Visitors: Anyday   Designer: Willie Park
Hillside moorland course with burns and river as hazards

Jedburgh (1892)

Dunion Road, Jedburgh, Roxburghshire TD8 6LA
Tel: 01835 863587   Fax: 01835 862360
Green Fee: ①   9 Holes   5555 yds   SSS: 67
Visitors: Anyday   Designer: Willie Park
Undulating scenic parkland course

Kelso (1887)

Golf Course Road, Kelso, Roxburghshire TD5 7SL
Tel: 01573 223259 or 223009 Fax: 01573 228490

Green Fee: ①   18 Holes   6046 yds   SSS: 69
Visitors: Anyday   Designer: James Braid
Flat parkland course

Lauder (1896)

Galashields Road, Lauder, Berwickshire TD2 6RS
Tel: 01578 722526   Fax: 01578 722526
Green Fee: ①   9 Holes   5910 yds   SSS: 69
Visitors: Anyday   Designer: Willie Park
Parkland course enjoying spectacular views over Lauderdale

Lilliardsedge (1999)

Lilliardsedge, Jedburgh, Roxburghshire TD8 6TZ
Tel: 01835 830271   Fax: 01835 830271
Green Fee: ①   9 Holes   5230 yds   SSS: 66
Visitors: Anyday   Designer: Souters
Undulating meadowland course

Melrose (1880)

Dingleton Road, Melrose, Roxburghshire TD6 9RF
Tel: 01896 822855 or 822391

Green Fee: ①   9 Holes   5562 yds   SSS: 68
Visitors: Weekdays   Designer: Unknown
Undulating wooded parkland course situated at the foot of Eildon Hills

Minto (1928)

Minto Village, Hawick, Roxburghshire TD9 8SH
Tel: 01450 870220   Fax: 01450 870126
Green Fee: ②   18 Holes   5542 yds   SSS: 67
Visitors: Anyday   Designer: Unknown
Undulating parkland course with panoramic countryside views

Muirfield (1891)

Muirfield, Gullane, East Lothian EH31 2EG
Tel: 01620 842123   Fax: 01620 842977
Green Fee: ⑥   18 Holes   6601 yds   SSS: 73
Visitors: Weekdays   Designer: Tom Morris
Excellent links course where 15 Open Championships have been played

Area 15

North Berwick (1832)

New Club House, Beach Road, North Berwick, East Lothian EH39 4BB
Tel: 01620 895040   Fax: 01620 890312   Pro: 01620 893233
Green Fee: ③   18 Holes   6420 yds   SSS: 71
Visitors: Anyday   Designer: MacKenzie Ross
Links course used for Open Qualifying. Hazards include the beach streams and low walls

Peebles (1892)

Kirkland Street, Peebles, Peeblesshire EH45 8EU
Tel: 01721 720197 Fax: 01721 724441 Sec: 01721 720099
Green Fee: ② 18 Holes 6160 yds SSS: 70
Visitors: Anyday Designers: James Braid/Harry S. Colt
Undulating parkland course with fine views

Roxburghe, The (1997)

Heiton, Kelso, Roxburghshire TD5 8JZ
Tel: 01573 450333 or 450331 Fax: 01573 450611

Green Fee: ④ 18 Holes 6925 yds SSS: 74
Visitors: Anyday Designer: Dave Thomas
Wooded and mature parkland course with water hazards

Rutherford Castle (1998)

West Linton, Peeblesshire EH46 7AS
Tel: 01968 661233 Fax: 01968 661233 Pro: 01968 661356
Green Fee: ① 18 Holes 6525 yds SSS: 71
Visitors: Anyday Designer: Bryan Moore
Challenging undulating parkland course with natural water hazards

St. Boswells (1899)

Braeheads, St. Boswells, Melrose, Roxburghshire TD6 0DE
Tel: 01835 823527

Green Fee: ① 9 Holes 5274 yds SSS: 66
Visitors: Anyday Designer: Willie Park (altered 1956 John Shade)
Scenic parkland course situated along the banks of River Tweed

Selkirk (1883)

Selkirk Hill, Selkirk, Selkirkshire TD7 4NW
Tel: 01750 20621
Green Fee: ①   9 Holes   5575 yds   SSS: 67
Visitors: Anyday   Designer: Willie Park
Moorland hilltop course overlooking the town

Torwoodlee (1895)

Edinburgh Road, Galashields, Roxburghshire TD1 2NE
Tel: 01896 752660   Fax: 01896 752660

Green Fee: ②   18 Holes   6021 yds   SSS: 70
Visitors: Anyday   Designer: Willie Park (new layout John Garner)
Scenic parkland course alongside River Gala

West Linton (1890)

Medwyn Road, West Linton, Peeblesshire EH46 7HN
Tel: 01968 660970   Fax: 01968 660970   Pro: 01968 660256
Green Fee: ②   18 Holes   6132 yds   SSS: 70
Visitors: Anyday   Designers: Braid/Millar/Fraser
Moorland course with views of the Pentland Hills

Whitekirk (1995)

Whitekirk, North Berwick, East Lothian EH39 5PR
Tel: 01620 870300   Fax: 01620 870330
Green Fee: ②   18 Holes   6526 yds   SSS: 72
Visitors: Anyday   Designer: Cameron Sinclair
Scenic coastal course with gorse and stunning views

Winterfield (1935)

North Road, Dunbar, East Lothian EH42 1AU
Tel: 01368 862564   Fax: 01368 862280   Pro: 01368 863562
Green Fee: ①   18 Holes   5155 yds   SSS: 64
Visitors: Anyday   Designer: Unknown
Public seaside links course in attractive coastal setting

Woll (1993)

Woll Estate, Ashkirk, Selkirkshire TD7 4NY
Tel: 01750 32222   Fax: 01750 32222
Green Fee: ①   9 Holes   6406 yds   SSS: 71
Visitors: Anyday   Designer: Unknown
Natural parkland course situated in the beautiful Woll Estate

Area 15

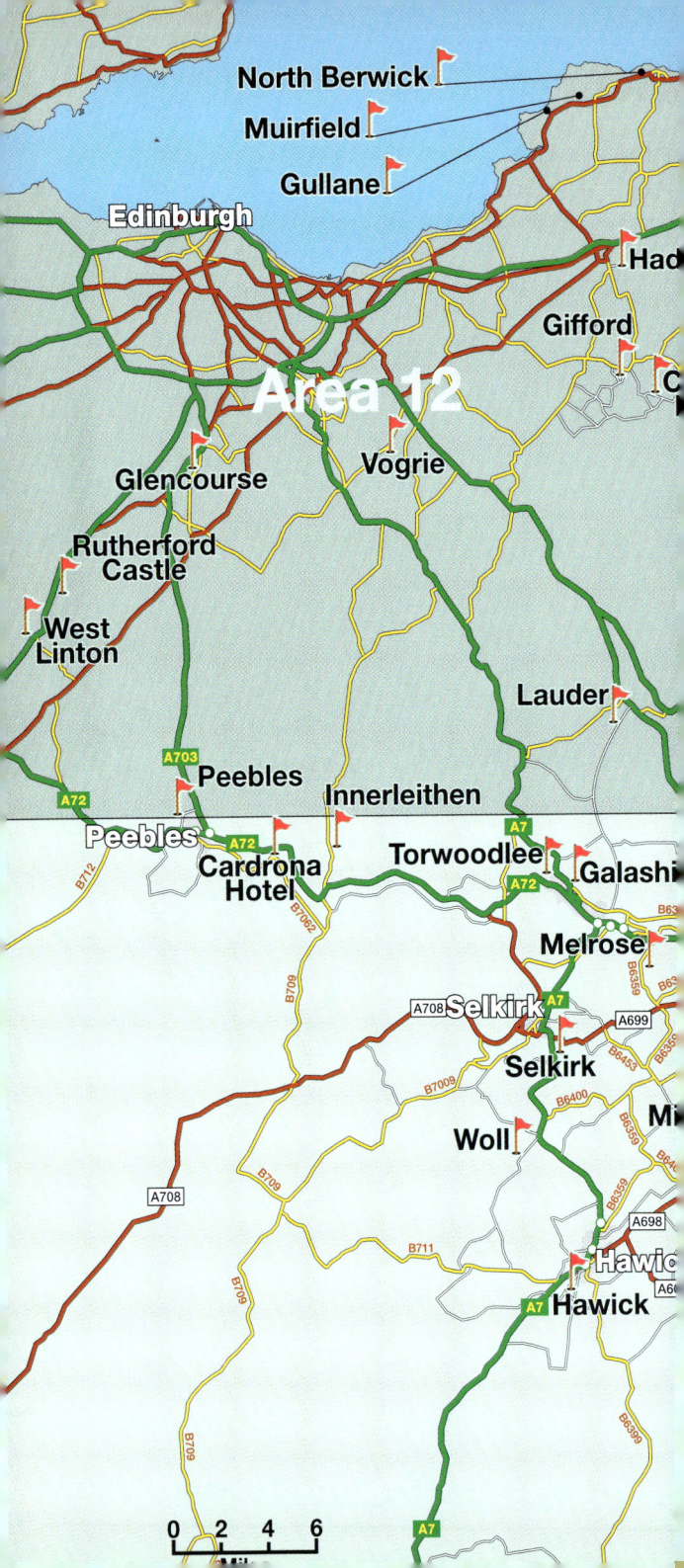

North Berwick

Muirfield

Gullane

Edinburgh

Had

Gifford

C

Area 12

Vogrie

Glencourse

Rutherford
Castle

West
Linton

Lauder

A703

Peebles

Innerleithen

A72

Peebles

A72

Cardrona
Hotel

Torwoodlee

A7

Galashi

A72

B712

B7062

Melrose

B63

B6353

B6359

B709

A708 Selkirk

A7

A699

B7009

Selkirk

B6453

B6355

A708

Woll

B6400

B6359

Mi

B709

B6400

B6459

A698

B711

B709

Hawick

A60

A7

Hawick

A698

B709

B6450

A7

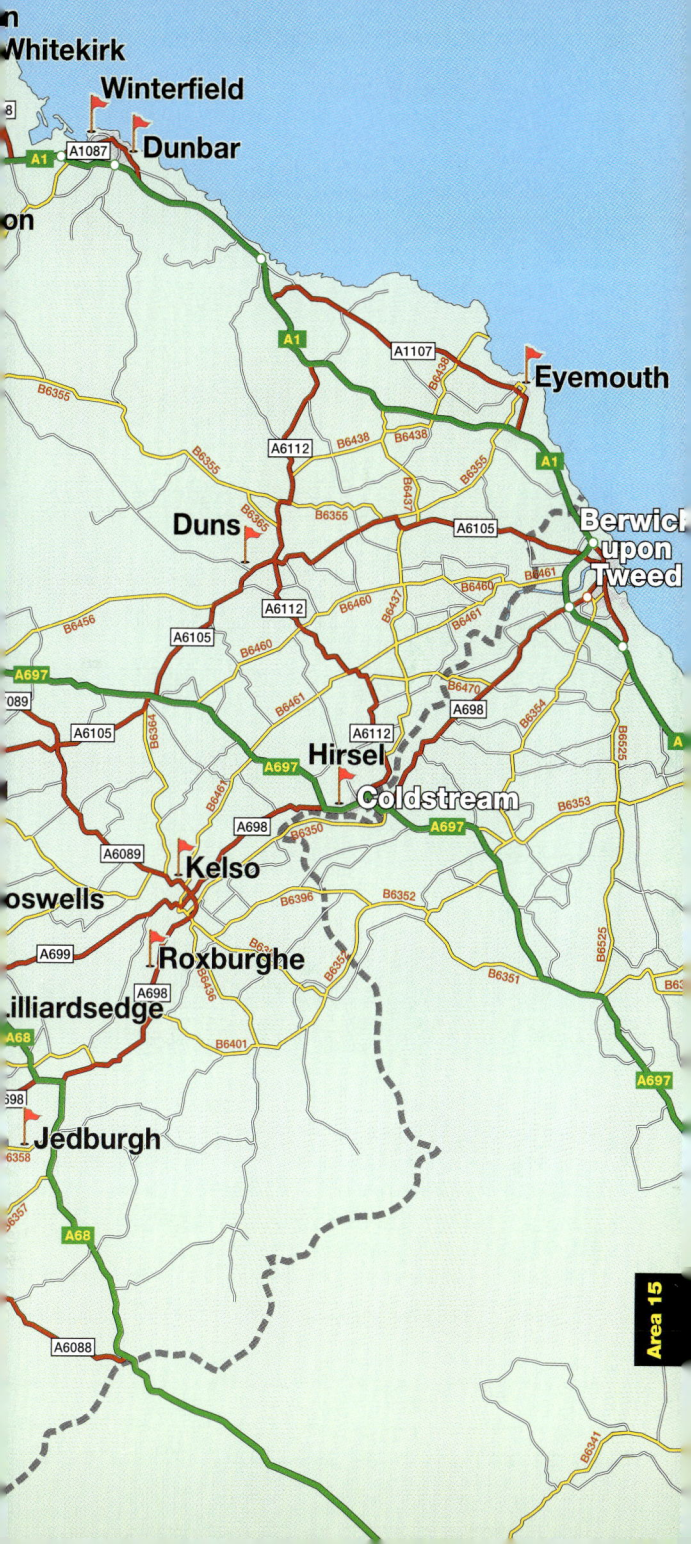

Whitekirk

Winterfield

A1087 Dunbar

A1

on

A1

A1107 Eyemouth

B6355

A6112 B6438 B6438

A1

B6355 B6438 B6355

Duns A6105 Berwick upon Tweed

A6112 B6460 B6457 B6460 B6461

B6456 B6460 A698

A6105 B6460 B6470

A697 B6461 A698 B6554 B6525

089 B6364 A6112 A697 A

A6105 A697 Hirsel B6353

A698 Coldstream

A6089 B6350 A697

Kelso B6396 B6352

oswells B6525

A699 Roxburghe B6351 B63

A698 B6355

illiardsedge B6401

A68

698 Jedburgh

6358

B6357 A68 A697

A6088

B6341

Area 15

Cally Palace Hotel (1994)

Gatehouse of Fleet, Dumfriesshire DG7 2DL
Tel: 01557 814341   Fax: 01557 814522

Green Fee: ①   18 Holes   5531 yds   SSS: 70
Visitors: Residents Only   Designer: Tom MacAuley

Part parkland/woodland course with pleasant views

Gatehouse of Fleet (1921)

Laurieston Road, Gatehouse of Fleet, Kirkcudbrightshire DG7 2BE
Tel: 01644 450260   Fax: 01644 450260

Green Fee: ①   9 Holes   5042 yds   SSS: 66
Visitors: Anyday   Designer: Unknown

Some stunning views from this parkland course

Kirkcudbright (1893)

Stirling Crescent, Kirkcudbright, Kirkcudbrightshire DG6 4EZ
Tel: 01557 330314   Fax: 01557 330314

Green Fee: ②   18 Holes   5739 yds   SSS: 69
Visitors: Anyday   Designer: Unknown

Parkland course with marvellous panoramic views of the Dee estuary

Lagganmore (1990)

Lagganmore Farm, Portpatrick DG9 9AB
Tel: 01776 810262   Fax: 01776 810499

Green Fee: ①   18 Holes   5698 yds   SSS: 69
Visitors: Anyday   Designer: Unknown

Pay and play course laid out on meadowland

New Galloway (1902)

New Galloway, Castle Douglas, Kirkcudbrightshire DG7 3RN
Tel: 01644 420737   Fax: 01644 450685   Sec: 01644 450685
Green Fee: ①   9 Holes   4540 yds   SSS: 67
Visitors: Anyday   Designer: James Braid
Hilly upland course. Haven for wildlife with unsurpassed views

Newton Stewart (1896)

Kirroughtree Avenue, Minnigaff, Newton Stewart, Dumfriesshire DG8 6PF
Tel: 01671 402172   Fax: 01671 402172

Green Fee: ②   18 Holes   5970 yds   SSS: 70
Visitors: Anyday   Designer: Unknown
Hilly parkland course in picturesque setting with magnificent views

Portpatrick (1903)

Golf Course Road, Portpatrick, Wigtownshire DG9 8TB
Tel: 01776 810273   Fax: 01776 810811

Green Fee: ②   18 Holes   5882 yds   SSS: 69
Visitors: Anyday   Designer: C. W. Hunter
Seaside links-style set on cliff. Wonderful views of Irish coast and Mull of Kintyre

Area 16

St. Meaden (1905)

Monreith, Newton Stewart, Wigtownshire DG8 8NJ
Tel: 01988 700358   Sec: 01988 500326
Green Fee: ①   9 Holes   4454 yds   SSS: 63
Visitors: Anyday   Designer: James Braid
Links course with panoramic views as far as the isle of Man

Stranraer (1905)

Creachmore, Leswalt, Stranraer, Wigtownshire DG9 0LF
Tel: 01776 870245   Fax: 01776 870445

Green Fee: ②   18 Holes   6308 yds   SSS: 72
Visitors: Anyday   Designer: James Braid (original course)
Moved to present site in 1953. Parkland seaside course with views of Arran and Ailsa Craig

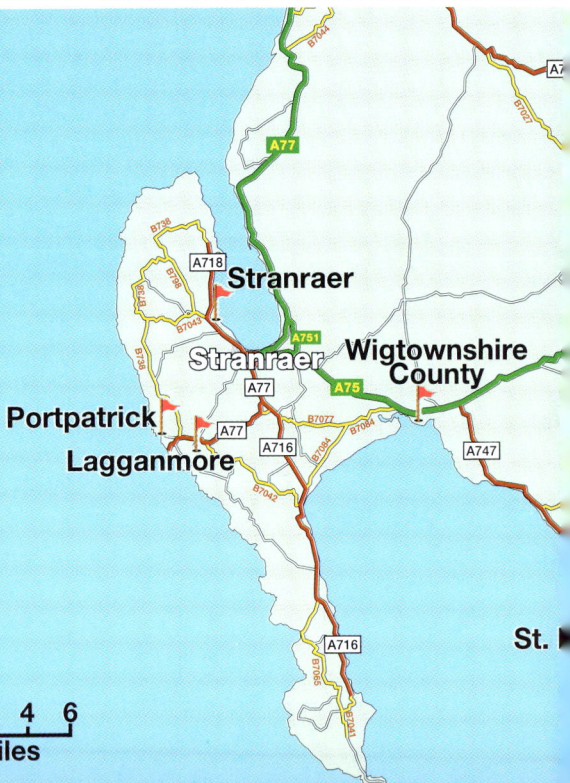

0 2 4 6
Miles

Wigtown & Bladnoch (1960)

Lightlands Terrace, Wigtown, Dumfriesshire DG8 9DY
Tel: 01988 403354

Green Fee: ①   9 Holes   5462 yds   SSS: 67
Visitors: Anyday   Designer: W. Muir

Hilly parkland course with views of the Galloway Hills and Wigtown Bay

Wigtownshire County (1894)

Mains of Park, Glenluce, Wigtownshire DG8 0NN
Tel: 01581 300420

Green Fee: ②   18 Holes   5847 yds   SSS: 68
Visitors: Anyday   Designer: Charles Hunter/G. Cunningham (new 9)

Easy walking seaside links course on the shores of Luce Bay

Brighouse Bay (1999)

Borgue, Nr. Kirkcudbrightshire DG6 4TS
Tel: 01557 870409   Fax: 01557 870409

Green Fee: (2)   18 Holes   6602 yds   SSS: 73
Visitors: Anyday   Designer: Duncan Gray

Pay and play links-type course with coastal undulations

Castle Douglas (1905)

Abercromby Road, Castle Douglas, Kirkcudbrightshire DG7 1BB
Tel: 01556 502801

Green Fee: (1)   9 Holes   5408 yds   SSS: 66
Visitors: Anyday   Designer: Unknown

Pleasant parkland course with fine views and modern clubhouse

Colvend (1905)

Sandyhills, Dalbeattie, Kirkcudbrightshire DG5 4PY
Tel: 01556 630398   Fax: 01556 630495   Sec: 01556 610878

Green Fee: (2)   18 Holes   4720 yds   SSS: 67
Visitors: Anyday   Designer: Willie Fernie, extended 1997 by J. Soutar

Hilly meadowland course offering panoramic views

Crighton (1884)

Bankend Road, Dumfries, Dumfriesshire DG1 4TH
Tel: 01387 247894   Fax: 01387 257616   Sec: 01387 247544

Green Fee: (1)   9 Holes   6168 yds   SSS: 69
Visitors: Anyday   Designer: Unknown

Pleasant views of Dumfries town from this parkland course

Dalbeattie (1897)

Maxwell Park, Dalbeattie, Kirkcudbrightshire DG5 4JR
Tel: 01556 611421   Fax: 01556 610311
Green Fee: ①   9 Holes   5710 yds   SSS: 68
Visitors: Anyday   Designer: Unknown
Hill and parkland course with wildlife and panoramic views

Dumfries County (1912)

Edinburgh Road, Dumfries, Dumfriesshire DG1 1JX
Tel: 01387 253585   Fax: 01387 253585   Pro: 01387 268918

Green Fee: ②   18 Holes   5928 yds   SSS: 69
Visitors: Anyday   Designer: Willie Fernie
Beautiful mature parkland course bordered by the River Nith

Dumfries and Galloway (1880)

2 Laurieston Avenue Dumfries, Dumfriesshire DG2 7NY
Tel: 01387 253582   Fax: 01387 263848   Pro: 01387 256902

Green Fee: ②   18 Holes   6325 yds   SSS: 71
Visitors: Anyday   Designer: Willie Fernie
Challenging parkland course set in rolling countryside

Gretna (1991)

Kirtleview, Gretna, Dumfriesshire DG16 5HD
Tel: 01461 338464 or 337362

Green Fee: ①   9 Holes   6430 yds   SSS: 72
Visitors: Anyday   Designers: Nigel Williams/Bothwell
Parkland course with wonderful views across to Cumbria

Hoddom Castle (1973)

Hoddom Bridge, Ecclefechan, Dumfriesshire DG11 1AS
Tel: 01576 300251   Fax: 01576 300757
Green Fee: ①   9 Holes   4548 yds   SSS: 66
Visitors: Anyday   Designer: Unknown
Mature public parkland course laid out beside the banks of River Annan

Langholm (1892)

Whitahill, Langholm, Dumfriesshire DG13 0JR
Tel: 013873 80673 or 81247
Green Fee: ①   9 Holes   6180 yds   SSS: 70
Visitors: Anyday   Designer: Unknown
Hard-walking hillside course with fine views

Lochmaben (1926)

Castlehill Gate, Lochmaben, Dumfriesshire DG11 1NT
Tel: 01387 810552

Green Fee: ①   18 Holes   5377 yds   SSS: 67
Visitors: Anyday   Designer: James Braid
Undulating parkland course surrounding Loch Kirk

Lockerbie (1889)

Corrie Road, Lockerbie, Dumfriesshire DG11 2ND
Tel: 01576 203363   Fax: 01576 203363

Green Fee: ①   18 Holes   5493 yds   SSS: 67
Visitors: Anyday   Designer: James Braid original 9
Parkland course with pleasant views

Newcastleton (1894)

Holm Hill, Newcastleton, Roxburghshire TD9 0QD
Tel: 01387 375257
Green Fee: ①   9 Holes   5748 yds   SSS: 68
Visitors: Anyday   Designer: J. Shade (1974)
Hilly and pleasant scenic course

Pines (1997)

Lockerbie Road, Dumfries, Dumfriesshire DG1 3PF
Tel: 01387 247444   Fax: 01387 249600

Green Fee: ①   18 Holes   5850 yds   SSS: 69
Visitors: Anyday   Designer: Duncan Gray
Public undulating course built on grazing land, woodland and heather

Powfoot (1903)

Cummertrees, Annan, Dumfriesshire DG12 5QE
Tel: 01461 700276   Fax: 01461 700276   Pro: 01461 700327

Green Fee: ②   18 Holes   6266 yds   SSS: 71
Visitors: Anyday   Designer: James Braid
Seaside course laid out close to the Solway estuary. Pleasant views

Solway Links (1995)

East Preston Farm, Nr. Southerness, Dumfriesshire DG2 8BE
Tel: 01387 880323 or 880623   Fax: 01387 880567
Green Fee: ①   18 Holes   4701 yds   SSS: 66
Visitors: Anyday   Designer: Gordon Gray
Public links-type course with pleasant countryside views

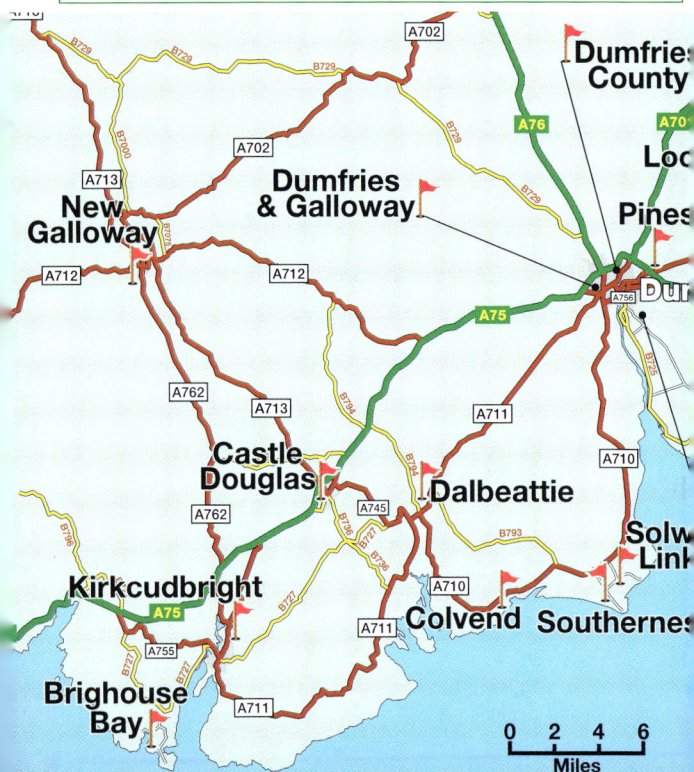

Southerness (1947)

Kirkbean, Dumfriesshire DG3 8AZ
Tel: 01387 880677   Fax: 01387 880644

Green Fee: ③   18 Holes   6566 yds   SSS: 72
Visitors: Anyday   Designer: MacKenzie Ross
*Natural links championship course with heather and
bracken*

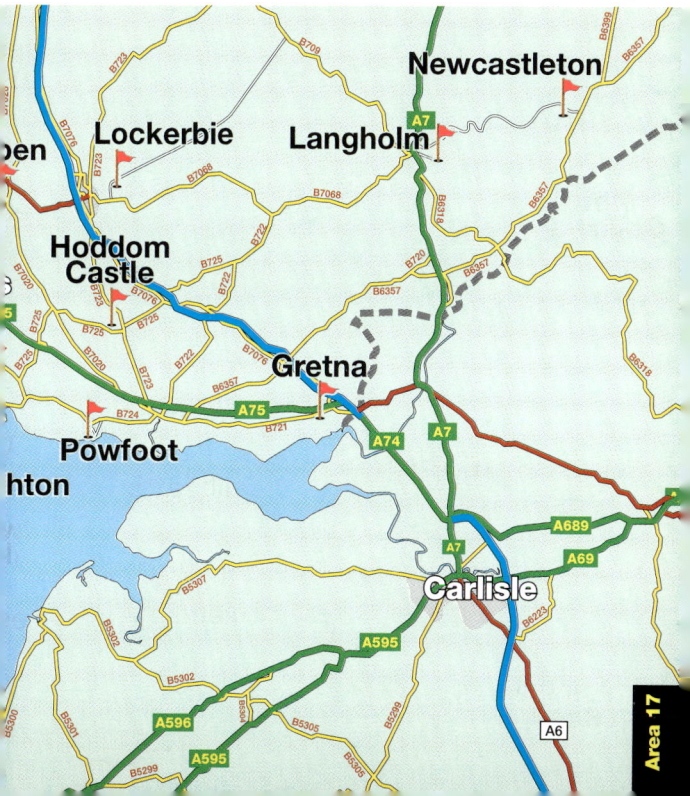

Newcastleton

Lockerbie   Langholm   A7

en

Hoddom
Castle

Gretna

Powfoot   A75

hton

A74   A7

A689

A7   A69

Carlisle

A595

A596

A595

A6

Area 17

ISBN 0-9539952-1-6

© Copyright 2002 Roger Kidd's Golf Guides

Origination by
Omnibus Graphics Ltd, Croydon, Surrey

Printed in Europe

Published by Roger Kidd's Golf Guides
26 Cedar Road,
Sutton,
Surrey SM2 5DG
Tel: 020 8643 0199

Every effort has been made to include all golf clubs in Scotland, but if you know of any clubs that have been missed please do not hesitate to contact Kidd's Golf Guides at the above address

Credits
St. Andrews and Turnberry Paintings by Terence Macklin

We would like to thank all the clubs that assisted us in the compilation of this book with information and pictures and the Scottish Tourist Board.

Area 1

Durness

A838

A837

Stornoway

Hebrides

Outer

Ullapool

A835

A

A82

Portree

A87

Skye

A87

For
Aug

Lochboisdale

A830

A86

Fort
William

A82

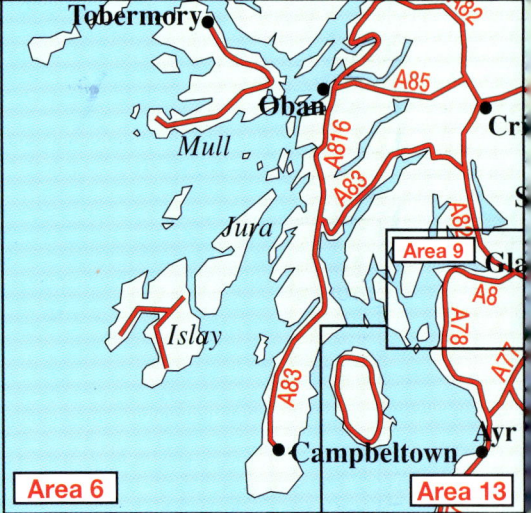

Tobermory

A82

A85

Oban

Cr

A816

Mull

A83

Jura

A82

Area 9

Gla

A8

Islay

A78

A7

A83

Ayr

Campbeltown

Area 13

Area 6

A7

Area 16

A7

Stranraer